Camelot... What It Was and How It Ended

The Assassination of President John F. Kennedy and the Tragedy that Followed

D1525547

Alexandra Amoroso

Yes, I know. Another book about John F. Kennedy. Why another JFK book? John F. Kennedy was the 35th President of the United States, who many Americans idolized. He was much more than a politician, he was a star, a beacon of hope for the future. He was a great public servant and a great patriot to the country. John Kennedy did so many great things during his short presidency. He kept us out of the war, promised to land a man on the moon and return him safely, launched the Peace Corps, and much more. Of course all that was shattered when he was gunned down in Dallas, Texas. Two days after Kennedy's death another gunshot left us with no answers. Why was Kennedy killed? Why was Oswald shot? However, we are left with some of these conspiracies.

Was it the mob?

A Cuban Plot?

A Russia Plot?

Was it the CIA?

Did Lee Harvey Oswald act alone?

More than five decades after the Kennedy assassination America is still left in the dark and everyone is haunted by the same question. Who killed John F. Kennedy? Here are some details about that tragic day, Lee Oswald and his suspicious behaviors, the Kennedy family and tragedy, and more. There are so many questions that are not answered. Was there a Kennedy curse?

Introduction

John Fitzgerald Kennedy was born on May 29, 1917 he was the second son and child to Joe and Rose Kennedy. John or Jack as they called him was one of nine children. There were four boys and five girls. He was born in Brookline Massachusetts. His paternal grandfather Patrick Joseph Kennedy was a member of the Massachusetts state legislative. John's maternal grandfather who he was named after, John F. Fitzgerald served as U.S. congressman and was elected as Mayor of Boston for two terms. All four of Kennedy's grandparents were children of Irish immigrants. In 1940 Kennedy served in the Navy and was awarded for his heroism when his PT boat was cut right in half by a Japanese destroyer. He later went on to Democratic politics after his brother Joe was killed in the war he was now the aspect of his father's political dynasty. He was congressman of Massachusetts and later was senator and while in the senate he met a beautiful young women Jacqueline Bouvier. The couple was married at St. Mary's Roman Catholic Church in Newport Rhode Island on September 12, 1953. Jackie's sister Lee was matron of honor, and JFK's brother Bobby served as best man. For their honeymoon John and Jackie spent two weeks in Acapulco, Mexico. After their honeymoon Jack confides to Jackie that he wants to become president. The couple had their first child Caroline in November of 1957. In 1960 Jack announces his candidacy for President of the United States. Kennedy ran against republican Vice President Richard Nixon and their debate was the first televised presidential debate. Kennedy beat Nixon and was president-elect. November 25, 1960 Jackie gave birth to their second child John F. Kennedy Jr. named after JFK. The family went down to their house in Palm Beach, Florida while Jack decided people he was choosing for his upcoming administration. On January 20, 1961 John F. Kennedy was sworn in as the 35th President of the United States by Justice Earl Warren in front of millions of Americans watching on that freezing cold day in January as President Kennedy stood there in just his dress jacket. The president stood before his people and stated words that are historical to this day. "And so my fellow Americans, Ask not what your country can do for you, ask what you can do for your country." After the ceremony was over the first family left for the White House. It's the most famous address in America. 1600 Pennsylvania Avenue. It is the home of the most powerful person in America and John F. Kennedy was now to live in that executive mansion. During their move to the White House Mrs. Kennedy found the desk that was given to President Rutherford B. Hayes by Queen Victoria stashed away it was called the resolute desk. It was brought out and used by Kennedy and his staff. John F. Kennedy believed his citizens should know what is going on with their country. He liked the news media and knew how to use it politically. The White House had a pool. JFK grew up on the water and often took breaks to go for a swim to help his back pain. Kennedy's aids and staff knew about his health problems and issues he had with his back they were very supportive and did everything they could to make the president more comfortable. The one thing Kennedy knew would help him and his presidency was to show his kids to the public eye. Jackie was very against that and didn't want her children in the public eye as much as she knew they would be. When Jackie Kennedy was away out of the country Kennedy said to his secretary Evelyn to go get his kids and bring them in the oval office. The kids came in and they danced and sang songs with Kennedy and he thought it was the best thing ever. The pictures got out and he was right the public fell all over them. The president knew how to persuade his people and he did it with the compassion and courage he had for his nation. Kennedy's presidency was truly one of the greatest things for our country. Camelot ended too soon when our beloved president was killed in an assassination in Dallas, Texas on November 22, 1963. The president and first lady were campaigning for his re-election in 1964 Air Force One landed in Dallas the President and First Lady walk off the plane what Kennedy didn't know was he only had an hour to live. Within that hour history made an unexpected turn. He was shot in Dealey Plaza around 12:30 that afternoon. John Fitzgerald Kennedy died at 1:00 on November 22, 1963 at Parkland memorial hospital after suffering gunshot wounds in an assassination he was buried at Arlington National Cemetery where to this day thousands of Americans go to visit each year. They also think about that shocking day in Dallas and who killed President Kennedy and why?

To the entire Kennedy family and the memory of the Kennedy brothers John and Bobby Kennedy who were great public servants.

Change is the law of life and those who only look to the past or present are certain to miss the future.

-John F. Kennedy

Chapters

Chapter 1

The Beginning of a New Era

January 20, 1961 it was a new decade with a lot of promise. John Fitzgerald Kennedy was elected into office as the 35 president of the United States. He was young, vigor, good looking, and a promising figure to our country. John Kennedy took the oath of office with courage, determination, and hope. He had hope for his family, his country, and the world. Pennsylvania Avenue had class like none other, it was no stranger to big eager crowds. When Pennsylvania Avenue was over the White House was next. The country was seeing a new president, a new waving hand, and a new administration. An administration that changed the country and made it a better place as John Kennedy promised to do. John F. Kennedy walked into that oval office ready to make change. Which he did, he accomplished a lot for the citizens of the United States. That is what he wanted to do was make a change that would be better for the American people. What the president did not know was his life was going to end in three years. The 1960 election with Kennedy and Nixon was a close one. Kennedy was very well liked by Democrats and Republicans. As most Americans say Joseph Kennedy bought him the presidency. Joe told Jack he wasn't paying for a landslide. The election between him and Nixon was a close one. JFK and his young family made our country look great. His presidency would soon be a rocky one when he faced the Bay of Pigs only three months after he had gotten elected and had to find some way to make Castro and Cuba back down. Kennedy swore he wanted no US military involvement and took the blame on national television when men were being killed and held as prisoners down there. This was after the Cuban

Revolution in 1959, when Castro forged strong economic links with the Soviet Union and at the time, the United States was engaged in the Cold War. When Kennedy was elected he had appointed many people to his administration. One of those people was his brother Robert "Bobby" Kennedy. He appointed his brother Bobby to attorney general where Bobby kept a close eye on Jack and stuck by him in times of crisis. However Kennedy's brother pursued a crusade against organized crime and the Mafia. Convictions against organized crime figures rose by eight hundred percent during his presidency. Bobby Kennedy worked to get FBI director J. Edger Hoover's focus away from communism, which Hoover saw as a threat to organized crime. The mobsters felt hounded by Bobby Kennedy and were angry that President John Kennedy didn't recover their Cuban playground. Kennedy appointed Lyndon Johnson as his vice president because he knew

Johnson was a very popular figure in Texas he needed Johnson to get in the White House even though Vice President Johnson and Attorney General Robert Kennedy despised each other. Jack reminded Bobby numerous times to be nice to Johnson and make him feel like he is very important to the administration. Bobby tried but you can still feel the tension when the both of them were in the same room together. Bobby would resign as Attorney General nine months after Jack dies. Jack knew he had to be President. When his father Joseph Kennedy's dream of becoming president went down the drain after the war in England and his older brother Joe died when his military plane exploded Jack knew it was up to him. Jack winning the presidency was the highlight of his father's life. Ambassador Kennedy had the political knowledge and the wealth to make it happen. His father was also willing to bend and break rules to get what he wants for himself and his family. He stuck by Jack's side and helped him deal with certain issues during his presidency but not long after Jack is president, his father suffers a massive stroke and is paralyzed on his right side. Kennedy was in trouble of October of 1962 when the United States was at the break of war with Cuba and the Soviet Union. Soviet Premier Nikita Khrushchev thought there was an opportunity for Cuba and the Soviet Union to strengthen their relationship. John Kennedy knew he had to act and do it quick, he had to find some way to persuade his country that the United States was fully prepared for war twelve thousand miles away. On October 22, 1962 Kennedy broadcasted his plan to deal with Cuba to the whole United States. He didn't want to do a full invasion in Cuba worried about causing a world war three and an airstrike would destroy all the missiles in Cuba. Kennedy and his cabinet decided to go ahead with a naval blockade. Within days the Soviets agreed to dismantle and remove all missiles in Cuba. Once again Kennedy kept America out of war. John Kennedy was famous for saying we can do better. The Kennedy White House was a brief period of political enchantment that came to be forever known as Camelot. He wanted the best for his country and only the best. What would John Kennedy do if he wasn't killed in Dallas? Would he appoint new people to his cabinet? Would he get voted in a second term? It's the questions that would haunt the country for decades to come. Kennedy's kids would only be able to spend a few years with their father until his life is taken by an assassin's bullet. Caroline Kennedy, six years old when her father was murdered spent the rest of her life with her mother and younger brother John Jr. she became an author, attorney, and diplomat who served as the United States Ambassador to Japan from 2013 to 2017. She has three children Rose, Tatiana, and Jack. John F. Kennedy Jr. was the prince of Camelot but America knew him simply as John-John. He was only three years old when his father passed away. Kennedy's funeral was held on November 25, 1963 the same day of John-John's third birthday who proudly saluted the father he would never know. He spent his early years in the White House and the public eye. After his mother passed away in 1994 John Jr. wanted to fly planes he got his license, which was always his dream. That dream led him to his death on July 16, 1999 when he, his wife Carolyn, and his sister-in-law Lauren set off at night to head to Martha's Vineyard for his cousin Rory Kennedy's wedding when his plane went down killing all three of them. As the wedding was canceled and the family was shocked of John's plane simply vanishing they all knew as days went by that they probably most likely did not survive. Even though it was many years after his father's tragic death in 1963 and his uncle's as well in 1968 it was devastating for the family to yet have another tragedy happen to them. President Kennedy got a lot done as president, he probably wanted to do more not only for his country but his family as well. They were a family full of charm and wealth, but faced tragedy like no other. By 1968 Joe and Rose Kennedy lost four of nine kids. It is reportedly called the "Kennedy Curse" but why the Kennedy's? They're an American family that people still question about every day. There are questions about their wealth, their power, and their lives. They lived lives most of us can only imagine, but also lives that were haunted by tragedy. It was Camelot. President Kennedy's assassination drew attention to millions of people.

Chapter 2

4 Days of Shock and Horror

On November 22, 1963 President Kennedy made a political trip to Texas, he knew he needed Texas to win the 1964 election and Kennedy was as unpopular in Texas as a president is likely to get. The trip was going great for him, the crowd was big everywhere. President and Mrs. Kennedy arrived in Dallas just before noon and the day couldn't be better, it was sunny the crowds were big and excited to see their president. Secret service knew President Kennedy would want the bubble top down because of the nice weather, which made them nervous. Jack and Jackie walked off air force one and right over to the crowd by the fence to greet them. This was something the President always did. He wanted to actually go up to the people and talk to them he knew that was the only way to get more votes. Secret service stayed close and kept watch carefully throughout the huge crowds. After shaking hands and talking to the crowd at Love Field, the President and Mrs. Kennedy get into the presidential motorcade not knowing that motorcade would lead the young president to his death. They were accompanied by Governor John Connolly and his wife Nellie. It was a beautiful day and the crowd couldn't get enough of John and Jackie they got such a warm welcome. The presidential motorcade made its way through downtown Dallas. Mrs. Kennedy looked beautiful in her bright pink suit and pink hat, she brought much joy to the people of Dallas seeing that she had accompanied the president on his campaign trip. The crowds got bigger as they made their way down Main Street as the crowds got big the car moved Kennedy away from the crowd which moved Mrs. Kennedy closer to the crowd. Her secret service agent Clint Hill stayed close to the motorcade for a while through the rest of Main Street, the car then made a right hand turn on Houston Street and slowed down to make a left hand turn onto Elm going slower because the crowds got smaller all of a sudden there was a loud bang which caught most people's attention including Governor Connolly, the secret service, and Mrs. Kennedy. The first lady had thought she heard a motorcycle backfiring, then there was a second bang which was the 1st bullet that hit the president in the back of the neck and exited through his throat and hitting Governor Connolly according to the Warren Commission.

President Kennedy grabbed at his throat and moved to his left violently. Governor Connolly had felt like someone hit him in the back with a doubled up fist, the force was so strong it pushed him forward and when he had looked down he was covered with blood. The 3rd shot is what forever changed history. The 3rd and fatal shot hits President Kennedy in the back of the head causing a small explosion, something that the people in Dealey Plaza that day will never forget seeing. Mrs. Connolly grabbed the governor and ducked down with him trying to keep him from losing blood. Mrs. Kennedy got back into her seat after grabbing a piece of the president's skull that had blown off his head when she sat in her seat the president's body fell into her lap and she admittedly grabbed his head and covered it so no one could see him. The car sped on to Parkland Memorial Hospital, President Kennedy and Texas Governor John Connolly are rushed into the hospital. President Kennedy's eyes were open, there was blood and brain all over him, the motorcade, and Mrs. Kennedy. In trauma room doctors and nurses strive to resuscitate him. It didn't look good at all, secret service and the doctors knew what was coming out of this. Meanwhile in Dealey Plaza Dallas Police surround the Texas School Book

Depository where eye witnesses say they heard numerous shots come from above towards the Book Depository. On the sixth floor there are three shell casings near a window with boxes set up that looked like a snipers perch, on the other side of the sixth floor behind some boxes a 30 caliber rifle was found as well as a snipers perch by one of the windows. After taking a headcount on all employees, all was there except one Lee Harvey Oswald. Dallas Police, shortly after the shooting gave out a description of the alleged suspect. While that is being done Oswald goes home to change his shirt and when he leaves his house this time he took his pistol with him. The search for him continued. Back at Parkland Hospital doctor, nurses, and the secret service saw no hope in saving the president's life. President Kennedy was declared dead at 1:00 central standard time. Everyone sat there in shock and disbelief as they looked around the trauma room at the blood all over the table, the floor, and on the doctors. They sat and looked down on their president who was laying there covered in his blood and brain tissue. They sat in silence for a little while wondering how and why did this happen. Mrs. Kennedy sat outside the trauma room covered in blood knowing her husband was gone. It was simply a tragic and horrific moment inside Parkland Hospital that day and for the citizens of Dallas. The one problem was transporting the President's body back to Washington because the law in Texas was if you are killed in Texas there has to be an autopsy done in Texas. The secret service did not care at all they were taking their president back to Washington where the autopsy will be performed there. A casket is brought to parkland and Mrs. Kennedy took off her wedding ring and placed it on the President's finger. Secret Service fought back and forth, pushing and shoving, doctors helped them get the president out and back to Washington. It was something no officer should argue. This was the President of the United States and they were taking him home. Finally they left the hospital and hurried to Air Force One where Vice President Lyndon Johnson and his wife Ladybird were waiting for the body and Mrs. Kennedy. Johnson became the 36th President of the United States, he didn't want the country to run without a functioning commander and chief. Johnson finished the oath, kissed Mrs. Kennedy and his wife, and then simply said, "Let's get this plane back to Washington." Then, Air Force One left for Washington. At 1:15 p.m. in the Oak Cliff section of Dallas Officer J.D Tippit is driving around listening to his radio for any updates on the suspect that murdered their president. While he is driving there is a man with a white jacket on walking towards him, the man suddenly turns around and walks the other way perhaps because he saw the police car. When Tippit approaches the man and asks where he is going the man replied he was just walking, but there was something about the guy that made Tippit want to get out of his car and talk to him face to face as he got out of his car the man pulled a pistol from his pants and shot the officer numerous times and then fled the scene throwing the empty cartages on the ground near the scene. There were a couple of witnesses who saw him pull the trigger and run, one man ran over to the police car and reported on the officers radio that he was shot. After this tragedy occurred there was a report over the radio that a man went into the Texas Theater without paying for a ticket. Police go into the Texas Theater and block all exits when a witness points the man out to them, they approach him and ask him to get up he gets up yelling "Well that's it, it's all over now" and as he does he punches one of the officers in the face and pulls out his pistol but another office gets hold of it and hits the man in the face right above his eye. As they get him out of the Texas Theater he was really putting up a fight kicking, yelling, and screaming. When they get the man in the car they ask him who he is, he doesn't reply so one of the officers takes his wallet and looks for a piece of identification he finds to ID's in the wallet one that say Lee H. Oswald and another that says Alex J. Hidell. Officers then decide to wait until they got to Police headquarters where he can be interpreted there by Captain J. W. Fritz. They get Oswald down to the Dallas City Jail and sit him in a room Captain Fritz comes into the headquarters and says he wants Officers to go out to a house in Oak Cliff and pick up a man by the name of Oswald when Fritz found out they already had him he started his first interrogation. Oswald flat out denies everything he is asked. The murder of President Kennedy, the murder of the officer, owning a rifle, he denies all of it. Dallas police knew they had evidence to connect Oswald to both shootings it was just the matter of making him crack. At 6:00 p.m. on Friday November 22nd Air Force One returns to Washington D.C carrying Vice President Lyndon Johnson, now the President of the United States and the body and remains of his former chief executive. Attorney General Robert Kennedy met

Mrs. Kennedy at the airport and both of them rode to the hospital in the ambulance with the casket. Johnson steps out in front of the press with his wife by his side and makes a brief statement saying, "I will do my best, that is all I can do, I ask for your help and God's." Back in Dallas, police try and figure out if Lee Harvey Oswald acted alone in killing President Kennedy or was part of some kind of international communist conspiracy they drove to Oswald's house out in Irving where his wife Marina lived with Ruth Paine and her two young daughters. When police arrived at the house Marina knew it had something to do with Lee. The rifle his wife claimed he owned was nowhere in the house. Marina knew Lee had to be involved in this. She went down to police headquarters with Oswald's mother Margaret the police brought the rifle to Marina to see if she could identify it. She was not a gun expert or knew what kind of rifle Lee owned. But she did know he had one that he made her order for him to a mailbox under the name of Alex Hidell. Captain Fritz and Dallas Police really thought that this was the guy that killed Kennedy but they needed a little more evidence to prove it and they need a confession. In Washington at the White House about 4:30 a.m. Saturday November 23rd John

Kennedy comes home for the last time he would lay in state there for the next day and then go to the Capitol on the 24th of November to lay in state there while people come pay their last respects for the young president. In the White House Mrs. Kennedy had the soldiers turn around and face JFK's casket instead of facing out so the president wouldn't feel alone. His chief of staff and official White House staff walked by the casket quietly to pay respects. There was a bright yellow sun that greeted Dallas on November 23rd but it greeted a different Dallas from the day before. While Lee Harvey Oswald is being questioned and dragged through all parts of the Dallas City Jail there is one man in the jail who is keeping watch throughout the whole scene, his name is Jack Ruby. Jack Ruby was a Dallas nightclub owner he owned the Carousel Club which he had closed for the weekend in honor of the President. He always loved to be where the action was and took it to heart when he heard President Kennedy was assassinated. Now because Ruby knew everyone and almost every officer in Dallas he walks in and out of the Dallas City Jail as he pleases. He was friends with a lot of officers and was able to get in the police headquarters plus with all the news station people there it was hard to see who came in and out. While Marina is home she is looking through old photos of happier times with Lee and the kids when suddenly she comes across a photo and it's of Lee Harvey Oswald holding a rifle with a pistol sticking out of his pants pocket. Marina knew she had to bring this to Dallas Police. When police showed Oswald the photo he said he didn't know anything about the photo every time he is questioned he denies, denies, denies. Every time flat out denial. Captain Fritz wasn't ready to give up. In Oswald's wallet he found a card that had his name on it that said, "Fair Play for Cuba Committee." Oswald didn't respond to it. Lee Harvey Oswald was a hard guy to crack. Oswald wouldn't admit to anything, he remained as calm as he could without breaking out into a sweat or trying to come up with an excuse, he was just so calm. How can a man be this calm when he just committed two crimes as police believed? That night Lee Harvey Oswald goes back to his jail cell which would be his last night sleep. The next morning November 24, 1963 John Fitzgerald Kennedy leaves the White House for the last time. Mrs. Kennedy wanted his funeral to be like President Lincoln's funeral nearly 100 years ago. President Kennedy's casket was brought to the Capitol Building where he would lay in

State for the public to view. People of Washington, citizens of America, and people all over the rest of the world mourn in shock and disbelief as they watched the President of the United States leave the White House in a casket. The casket is carried to the Capitol building and the only sound heard throughout the streets of Washington was the beat of the drums. Not one word was spoken and no one moved. Citizens simply stood and watched their once young and vigor president being carried through the streets of Washington in a coffin. Back in Dallas Lee Harvey Oswald is sitting in Captain Fritz's office waiting to be transferred from city jail to county jail. In the basement of the city jail news reporters and cameramen are all downstairs waiting to see and question the alleged assassin before he is transferred. In the group of reporters and newsmen there was Dallas nightclub owner Jack Ruby. Why? Because Jack Ruby who likes to be where all the action is saw they were transferring Oswald and wanted to go get a closer look. Did Ruby walk into the jail knowing he was going to shoot Oswald? No one knows. With his suit and hat on he looked like he was a reporter himself. Now Ruby had been seen in the county jail all weekend, it didn't occur to the police officers and reporters there that he was any threat to Oswald. Oswald comes downstairs in a black sweater walking with two detectives and is handcuffed to one of them. Detective Jim Lavelle. Oswald approaches reporters who are ready with questions when suddenly Ruby jumps out of the crowd with his colt and pulls the trigger right in front of Oswald, shooting him in his lower abdominal. He screamed in pain and fell to the floor. Ruby is brought upstairs in police custody. As President Kennedy is on his way to the Capitol where he would lie in state, Oswald is on his way to Parkland Memorial Hospital same place where Kennedy died two days ago. He is rushed to trauma room two because doctors did not want Oswald to die in the same room as the president. They opened up his chest and began to massage his heart by hand. They did absolutely everything they can, but were unsuccessful. At 1:07 p.m. Sunday November 24, 1963 Lee Harvey Oswald dies just 48 hours and 7 minutes after President John F. Kennedy. It was the murder that would haunt our country for decades to come. Now we will never really know what actually happened on the shocking day in Dallas. The big question now is what kind of man shot Lee Oswald and why? Was the CIA? The Mob? A Russian Plot? A Cuban Plot? The new

President Lyndon Johnson ordered these questions answered. He reported a Commission of seven men to investigate and make a report on the murder. After 9 months of investigating the Warren Commission report was made with over 800 pages. They came to their final conclusion that Lee Harvey Oswald acted alone and no one else was involved. Fifty- years later and no one is really sure what actually happened. Even though the Warren Commission concluded that Oswald acted alone in killing Kennedy the real truth about Kennedy's assassination is still a mystery. Could Oswald have been innocent? Not too many people believe Oswald was innocent because he certainly didn't look innocent. There is simply too many questions that still haven't been answered. Whoever killed President Kennedy never went to trial and never went to jail. He was killed right in the middle of the streets of Dallas, his alleged killer was murdered two days later and there was no one else they had to put on trial for Kennedy's assassination. In other words was Lee Harvey Oswald killed to shut his mouth? On November 25, 1963 President Kennedy and Lee Harvey Oswald were buried within hours of each other. The funeral of John Kennedy was held on the same day of his beloved son John Jr.'s third birthday who touchingly saluted the father he would never know. At 3:13 p.m. on that cold November day John F. Kennedy was laid to rest. For the next five decades there are questions and concerns about both murders. Day by day the confusion of doubt grew deeper. What really happened on November the 22nd 1963?

Chapter 3

The Mafia and the Kennedy's

John F. Kennedy was very connected with the mob as was his father Joseph Kennedy. Thanks to his former buddy Frank Sinatra, and the biggest mobster in America Sam Giancana, he would have never won Chicago like he did. Sinatra and Giancana were best friends. Giancana was also friends with Jack Ruby. Could the mob have Kennedy killed and then hired Jack Ruby to kill the president's alleged assassin to silence him? For starters, Sam was the crime boss of Chicago. There is a lot of evidence that proves the mob hated both John Kennedy and Bobby Kennedy and that they were involved not only with President Kennedy's murder but others as well. In 1960 during President Kennedy's campaign his father Ambassador Joe Kennedy met with Frank Sinatra and Sam Giancana about the polls in Chicago both men told Ambassador Kennedy he would do just fine and they wish John luck in his election. Frank Sinatra and John Kennedy had some fun times in Vegas together and Sinatra wanted John to become president because he wanted a president for a pal. Joseph Kennedy got Sam to help him with all his money and his connections. Sam also saved Joe Kennedy's life on another occasion. Joe Kennedy insulted Frank Castillo and Castillo was going to have Joe Kennedy killed; Joe contacted Sam Giancana and he saved Joe Kennedy. Kennedy and Nixon came very close but JFK won and was headed for the White House. In Kennedy's Administration his brother Robert "Bobby" Kennedy was appointed as Attorney General. Bobby Kennedy pursued a relentless crusade against organized crime and the Mafia. Kennedy was relentless in his pursuit of Teamsters Union president Jimmy Hoffa due to Hoffa's known corruption in financial and electoral matters, both personally and organizationally. The relationship between the two men was intense. After seeing his speech on TV against organized crime, Giancana called Sinatra and blasted him about Kennedy, Sinatra told him not to worry it will pass and he'll handle it. Sinatra called Joe Kennedy and told him Giancana was going crazy and he was furious with Bobby over the organized crime. Joseph Kennedy yelled at Sinatra for putting his family in danger, he told him to never talk to any of them ever again. Joe called Bobby and tried to convince him to maybe start small. Don't go after the big mobsters. Bobby who wasn't afraid or seemed fazed by his father's advice told him he can handle the big mobster's just fine. Of course Joe didn't want to try and tell Bobby what to do with his job so he left him to do what he was doing with the organized crime. The Mafia needed both John and Bobby out of office to keep them from going after them, but what made Sam even madder was when Bobby Kennedy got New Orleans boss Carlos Marcello deported to Guatemala and that was the last straw for Sam. He really wanted to destroy Sinatra who promised him the whole time that Kennedy could be trusted. Giancana loved Frank Sinatra too much to kill him. Giancana had said, "If Sinatra didn't sing Chicago as good as he did, I would have had him killed." The Mobsters felt hounded by Attorney General Robert Kennedy and were angry that President John Kennedy didn't recover their Cuban playground. Oswald's accused assassin Jack Ruby was popular and close with the mob. Ruby could have been paying off an IOU the day he was used to kill Oswald, and Lee Oswald had a huge connection with Cuba. Ruby stated to Chief Justice Warren in their 1964 session that he was used for a purpose. It would not have been hard for the mob to maneuver Ruby through the ranks in the Dallas

Police headquarters to kill Lee Oswald. With no Lee Oswald there is no alleged assassin to open their mouth in court and tell the truth of the assassination which is what the mob probably wanted. Before Kennedy's political trip to Dallas, FBI director J. Edger Hoover scolded Kennedy about having an affair with Judith Campbell Exner who was also having an affair with Sam Giancana at the same time. He ended the affair to keep the peace with the FBI. Did Kennedy and Sam know they were sharing the same women? It was dangerous for him to being doing that when Campbell was having an affair with one of the biggest mobsters in America. The fact that Bobby Kennedy was investigating him for his organized crime scared both the FBI and Bobby because Jack was having an affair with Campbell. Kennedy's assassination wasn't the only murder that was questioned as being a mob murder. There were questions and concerns about the death of Marilyn Monroe in 1962. Monroe had slept with John Kennedy, Bobby Kennedy, Frank Sinatra, and Sam Giancana. Bobby Kennedy was trying to end the affair with Marilyn because she was becoming unstable. There were times when John Kennedy left events during the White House by having an aid tell him there was a problem he needed to look at and he would leave to go sit in the White House theater with Marilyn Monroe. Sam knew her before she became famous. She was one of the most popular sex symbols of the 1950's and had a complete obsession with President Kennedy, begging Bobby Kennedy to let her speak to him because Jack wanted her and not Jackie. Bobby thought she was crazy. She thought Kennedy was going to leave Jackie for her, it made Bobby furious and he asked Marilyn to never contact him again. It was said that Monroe died of a drug overdose but within the following decades, several conspiracy theories including murder were talked about after Monroe's shocking death. Was it the Mob? They knew the affair Kennedy and Monroe had and being the biggest sex symbol she was it probably was murder and not suicide. Sam learned from Monroe that she had love letters from Bobby Kennedy. Sam's alleged plan according to his brother, kill Monroe and make it look like a suicide with the love letters to Bobby Kennedy beside her so he would get blamed, but Bobby wasn't blamed at all. Secret service got to the scene before police did and removed all of Bobby's love letters from the scene. Did Sam's plan to get back at Bobby Kennedy backfire? With that and Bobby also going after the Mob was enough for

Sam. He wanted the Kennedy's out of the White House, Sam couldn't trust them at all. All these people who were involved or allegedly involved with all these murders all had some kind of connections with the Mafia. In other words they were all killed to be silenced. Was Monroe killed to silence her about her love affairs with John Kennedy, Frank Sinatra, and Sam Giancana? Now the public has no idea why and how they were all murdered and what they knew before they were killed. Monroe wasn't what the FBI was worried about. Judith Campbell claimed to be having an affair with both Giancana and JFK and that they delivered communications between both of them about Fidel Castro. Giancana's daughter Antoinette Giancana stated her belief that her father was performing a scam to get millions of dollars of the CIA funding. On February 7, 1960 Frank Sinatra and Judith Campbell were in Las Vegas, where he introduced her to Senator and Presidential Candidate John F. Kennedy. Two months after Sinatra introduced her to JFK he then introduced her to "Sammy" Sam Giancana. She became very involved with Giancana and Kennedy. In Campbell's 1977 Memoir she wrote that she became one of Kennedy's mistresses for about two years, while he was president. She continuously visited him at the White House. Kennedy's actions with Campbell made it pretty clear that the mob hated the Kennedy's and wanted them out of the government to save the mob. You have two big political figures in the government John Kennedy and Robert Kennedy, who the mafia particularly despised and it is very clear that they despised Bobby with their meetings about the organized crime where Giancana laughed at Bobby Kennedy when he tried calling him out on certain things. John Kennedy was having an affair with a girl who was also having an affair with one of the biggest mobsters in America probably to get information out of JFK for the mob and vice versa. Before Kennedy can even get re-elected he is shot and killed and two days later the man Dallas Police believed killed him was gunned down by a man who was popular, well-known, and had connections with people in the Mafia. All this information put together can clearly show everyone that the Mob could have had a very close connection in the Kennedy Assassination. Why would anyone kill the man that investigators think shot our President? Wouldn't they want to know why Oswald did it? Everyone knew that President Kennedy picked Lyndon Johnson to be his Vice President because he was a very powerful political figure from Texas and Kennedy needed Texas in order to win the Presidency. He picked Robert Kennedy for Attorney General because he was his right hand man and both Jack and his father Joe wanted Bobby there to keep an eye out for Jack. It was very clear to John Kennedy, the Kennedy family, the Kennedy administration, and the country that Lyndon Johnson and Bobby Kennedy hated each other. They couldn't stand one another. Bobby found Johnson to be a very arrogant Vice President and Johnson felt the same way towards Bobby because he knew in 1968 Bobby would follow in Jack's footsteps for the Democratic Nomination. November 22, 1963 Kennedy is killed and pronounced dead at one o'clock p.m. almost two hours later Lyndon Johnson is sworn in as the 36th President of The United States. If there was one thing everyone knew it was that Robert Kennedy would not stay and serve as Attorney General under the Johnson Administration. Bobby stayed for nine months after his brother was killed and then left for the Senate election in New York in 1964 so by September of 1964 the Mafia was free; Kennedy was dead and Robert Kennedy left office. There is another Presidential election coming up in 1968 and Robert Kennedy is one of the nominees running for office. Six months in Bobby is shot and killed by an assassin's bullet. Both Kennedy's are dead and unable to go after the mob and their organized crime. Was Oswald the guy who killed Kennedy and did not know two days later he be silenced forever? Oswald told Dallas police that he was just a "patsy." That can be a true statement that Oswald was used to kill Kennedy by some conspiracy. A scary connection was Lee Harvey Oswald's uncle was Carlos Marcello's lieutenant. The other question is was Jack Ruby being used as well? Was Jack Ruby who always liked to be the center of attention used by the mob? It is possible and he would of course take the job. Questions were also raised when Sam Giancana was killed in the basement kitchen of his house while he was frying sausage and peppers. He was shot multiple times in the back of the neck and the suspect flew from the scene. Did the mob have plan to kill Giancana? Why didn't Sam have any of his bodyguards with him? The mob is a big question in this situation. It is very clear that Lee Harvey Oswald was a patsy and both Oswald and Jack Ruby were part of a conspiracy and an official cover-up to keep the public from learning the truth. Ruby and Sam were friends. Did he order Jack Ruby to kill Oswald to make sure he would never talk? Jack Ruby later died in 1967 of lung cancer. Did Ruby know he was going to die? Did it matter if he went to prison for killing Lee Harvey Oswald? Sam Giancana put the problem on Jack Ruby to take care of the situation. Sam had every desire to be in the public eye and to be famous. He knew the Kennedy's would just destroy him. What many of us know if anyone out there wanted President Kennedy dead more than anyone it was mobster Sam Giancana. Reportedly Frank Sinatra admitted to his daughter Tina the last years of his life that he had arranged a meeting between Sam Giancana and Joe Kennedy to meet in Hyannis Port about the Mafia issue. What would be in it for Sam? Well for one thing Bobby Kennedy would lay off, John Kennedy would focus on the Soviet Union and lay off organized crime and Sam could operate freely knowing that he owned the White House. Something about all this sounded good to Sam. Will we ever find out that the Mafia was the conspiracy involved? With Kennedy's affairs taking place with some of the most famous women connected with the mob it definitely caused a stir in the Kennedy White House. It simply made it harder for FBI director J. Edgar Hoover who was watching these women and for Bobby Kennedy who was investigating the crime boss of Chicago. JFK's affairs spelled out danger. President Kennedy had been sleeping with hookers who also shared a bed with some of the biggest mobsters being investigated for organized crime by JFK's brother Bobby. If Hoover and Bobby didn't stop it, it could have ended the Kennedy presidency, but John F. Kennedy once again got away with it. The Kennedy's and the Mafia... Well, they had history.

Chapter 4

Lee Harvey Oswald

Lee Oswald was a 24 year old ex-marine who was a big believer in Communism. He moved from house to house in different states multiple times, as a kid he was shown to be a poor student in school. After school he joined the Marines and became a sharp shooter; right before he was dishonorably discharged he was rated as a marksman. Oswald defected to the Soviet Union in October 1959. He lived in Russia until 1962 with his wife Marina in Belarusian City of Minsk. In 1962 they moved to the United States and finally settled in Dallas, Texas. Oswald was a huge supporter of President Castro and Cuba. He was arrested for disturbing the peace in New Orleans when he was handing out flyers that said "Fair Play for Cuba". He ordered the following items from a local printer: 500 application forms, 300 membership cards and 1,000 leaflets. He was handing them out in New Orleans where he was fined ten dollars after getting into a fight with a citizen from Cuba who was telling him Castro is nothing but a killer. Lee supported Cuba because it was the only country that was known for Marxism. In March of 1963 Lee Oswald purchased a 6.5 mm Caliber rifle by mail order using the name A.J. Hidell as well as a 38 Smith and Wesson model revolver by the same method. If Oswald supported Communism so much why did he join the Marines? Why didn't he live in Cuba and help Castro? On April 10, 1963 Lee Oswald was on a mission to kill retired U.S Major General Edwin Walker. Walker was a racist against Civil rights and wanted Kennedy to invade Cuba and overthrow Castro. Lee Oswald found out his address and went there with his 30 caliber rifle and fired his rifle at Walker through the window of his home, less than one-hundred feet away, as Walker was sitting at his desk. Walker only suffered minor injuries. Oswald's wife Marina testified that her husband told her he took a bus to Walker's house and shot at him with his rifle. Oswald stated he considered Walker to be a leader of a fascist organization. A month before Kennedy's arrival in Texas, Lee Harvey Oswald got a job as a clerk at the Texas School Book Depository. It was a six-story building in view of Dealey Plaza where President Kennedy spent his very last moments. The night before the assassination Oswald goes to his wife Marina's house for the night instead of Friday because he had to pick up curtain rods. Oswald stayed at Marina's house typically on Friday nights to spend the weekend with his two young daughters. The next morning on November 22nd Oswald left for work leaving money and his wedding ring behind. Into the Book Depository he carried a long paper package with him that Oswald claimed to have curtain rods in. Around 12:00 p.m. President Kennedy's motorcade was making its way down Main Street. Everyone at the Texas Book Depository made their way outside around that time to get a good look at the president. Oswald stayed inside during that time and had his lunch inside the Book Depository on the 6th floor where he was working. At around 12:30 p.m. three shots rang out in Dealey Plaza hitting both the President and Governor Connolly. People turned behind them where they heard the shots which was where the Depository building was. Police started running into the Book Depository where numerous people heard the shots. They surrounded the Texas School Book Depository while Captain Fritz took a head count of all the employees. Every employee was there except for one and that was Lee Harvey Oswald. They start to give out a description of the suspect to all squad cars. According to Oswald's landlord he came home in a hurry, he grabbed a jacket and his pistol and left. He started to walk through the Oak Cliff section of Dallas where Police Officer J.D Tippit pulled over and started to ask him questions. Tippit felt as though he had to get out of his car and look at the suspect eye to eye to talk to him; as he did that Oswald pulled his pistol from his pants and shot the officer multiple times leaving a bunch of empty shells behind. He then took off and ran inside the Texas Theater. He walked in the theater and didn't have a ticket. When he passed the ticket taker, she then called police to tell them she had a suspect come in the Texas Theater without purchasing a ticket. Dallas Police knew that sounded like the guy they were looking for. Within minutes Dallas Police surround the Texas Theater; they went in every door and they approached Oswald. They grabbed him but struggled to get him out, he really put up a fight but they finally got him into a Police cruiser. They take Oswald into Police custody and they find out he had two identification cards on him, one said Lee H. Oswald and the other one said A.J. Hidell. Dallas Police later learned that the rifle found in the Texas School Book Depository and Oswald's pistol were both purchased by mail order under the name A.J. Hidell. Oswald seemed to be a very arrogant person. He looked guilty of murder and his background showed what a guilty, arrogant, and cocky person he really was. What would life be like today if Oswald actually made it to his trial? The whole country was anxious to find out who Oswald really was and what his motive was. Dallas Police were certain that this was their guy. This was the guy that shot Officer Tippit and could have assassinated John Kennedy. Oswald's wife Marina went down to Police headquarters and told police that her husband did own a gun. Lee told reporters that were in the hall that he was just a patsy, but Captain Fritz couldn't get him to confess that he shot President Kennedy. They had enough evidence to connect Oswald to the Tippit shooting and almost enough to connect him to Kennedy's killing as well. The only evidence they found on the gun was a smudged palm print after Oswald died. Everything the police showed Oswald or questioned him about he denied it every time, straight denial. Police Chief Jesse Curry was certain this was the man who killed President Kennedy and he thought that he should be transferred that weekend to the county jail because it was a safer place to keep Oswald until trial. He decided to transport Oswald that Sunday morning. On November 24,

1963 Oswald wakes up and is brought to Captain Fritz's office for one more interrogation. Again, flat out denial to everything he was asked. Fritz decided to go ahead with the transfer and he would just interrogate Oswald later. Oswald was handed a black sweater to wear for the transfer because it was cold outside then he was handcuffed to detective Jim Leavelle. They headed down the elevator and were headed for the basement of the Dallas city Hall where reporters were to question Oswald before his transfer. Jack Ruby who was in the Dallas city jail all weekend watching Oswald's actions sneaks in through the basement and walks down the ramp to take a look himself. Did Ruby have a plan to kill Oswald? The elevator doors open and out walks Captain Fritz looking for his car to transfer Lee Oswald and behind him came Oswald escorted by two detectives. Oswald approaches the reporters and was headed for the car when Ruby jumps from the crowd, pulls his pistol out and pulls the trigger right in front of Oswald in his lower abdomen. Oswald yells in pain and falls to the ground. Jack Ruby is handcuffed and brought upstairs to the jail. Oswald is put into an ambulance and rushed to Parkland Hospital where President Kennedy died two days before. He is rushed to trauma room two across the hall where John F. Kennedy was being treated on Friday. Doctors opened his chest and started massaging his heart by hand, they desperately tried to save Oswald but they failed. Was Oswald an alone gunman? Or was he part of a conspiracy? Lee Harvey Oswald a 24-year old ex-Marine, big believer in Communism, and alleged Presidential assassin was murdered before we can learn what he knew. Now more than 50 years later, the mystery of Kennedy's assassination still remains strong. What really took place in Dealey Plaza on November the 22' 1963? Could Oswald have been the assassin? Yes. Oswald's background says a lot about communism, Russia, and his past events where he attempted an assassination tells how arrogant he was. Was Oswald being set up to kill Kennedy by the mob or the Cuban Embassy? The answer to that will forever be silent. Lee Harvey Oswald will always be a figure of mystery.

Chapter 5

Jack Ruby

Jack Ruby know as Jacob Rubenstein always liked being
the center of attention and being the big shot. Ruby was
the owner of two strip clubs Carousel Club in downtown
Dallas and the Vegas Club in the city's Oak Lawn district.
Ruby was friends with everyone he knew every Police
officer in Dallas and more. On November 22, 1963 Ruby
was at the Dallas Police station getting a close look at the
suspect he was also handing Cards out to news reporters
to come to get free drinks at his club. Ruby closed the
Carousel Club for the weekend in memory of President
Kennedy. Police knew Ruby and he was dressed just like a
news reporter so he looked like he fit in. He was there all
weekend watching every move Oswald made. Was Ruby
being used to kill Oswald or was it a last minute decision?
Jack Ruby had questionable connections, he had helped
out his BFF Sam Giancana for many years. Giancana
remember Ruby and kept him in mind for future help. The
morning of November 24, 1963 Lee Oswald is brought
down to the basement of the police station to be

transferred. It was the morning when another gunshot made a terrible situation even worse. Jack Ruby appears in the crowd and leaps out and pulls his trigger right up against Oswald. Oswald falls to the floor in pain and Ruby is brought upstairs into police custody. Ruby simply stated: "I couldn't help it." Was Ruby being paid by the Mob to end the Kennedy assassination investigation? Jack Ruby was known for being the center of attention and being the big shot, but why would he be the one to silence the alleged suspect. Jack Ruby knew what he was getting into and he knew Oswald had to be silenced and quick. Almost every Police officer knew Jack Ruby because he was a local nightclub owner in Dallas, because Ruby was good friends with almost all of them he was able to get into the Dallas City jail. Ruby later died of cancer. On March 14, 1964 the jury reached their verdict in the famous Jack Ruby murder trial. Ruby was found guilty of murder with malice and sentenced to death. In 1965 Ruby died of lung cancer. The jury said that this was the greatest railroading kangaroo court disgrace in the history of American law.

Chapter 6

Is there a Kennedy Curse?

Joseph and Rose Kennedy were married in 1914 both came from political families, Rose's father was former Mayor of Boston and Joe Kennedy's father was Senator of Massachusetts. Over the next eighteen years Joe and Rose raise nine children four girls and five boys. By the age of 25 Joe Kennedy became one of the youngest bank presidents in America. He made millions on Wall Street, Hollywood, and in the liquor trade. In 1938 President Franklin D. Roosevelt made Joe Kennedy Ambassador to Great Britain it was a triumph not only for Joe but his entire family. There was no doubt that Joe Kennedy had political ambitions, including one day to become president. Although Joe's political dreams were big, his young family was also ready to step into politics even at young ages. Even his youngest son Teddy at age six wasn't camera shy. Joe's oldest daughter Rosemary was special needs back then in that generation Joe referred to her as mentally disturbed. He feared her random outbursts and misbehavior would ruin his other children's careers especially the ones entering politics. It is sad to see Joe think that of one of his children. In those days it was different he thought Rosemary's outbursts should stop on their own. Doctors explained to Mr. Kennedy that his daughter will never advance above an eight year old. In 1941 Joe had arrange for his oldest daughter Rosemary to undergo a lobotomy, her mood swings and behavior was starting to scare Kennedy and he really only wanted the best for his daughter. Doctors said it would help keep Rosemary calm. The procedure was done but his wife Rose was not informed about it until the procedure was completed. Tragically the operation failed leaving Rosemary institutionalized for the rest of her life. Kennedy's second son John turned his senior thesis from school into a book called, "Why England Slept" while his father was dealing with the war as ambassador his book was the foundation of his political career. With his father's wealth and connections, he helped make it a best seller. While John's political career gets launched, Joe Kennedy's takes a hit. As England fights for its life Joseph Kennedy tells an American reporter that democracy is finished in England and may be in the United States as well. His remark turns both countries against him and Joe is recalled as Ambassador. It ends his political career and his dream of one day becoming president. His eldest son Joe Jr. knew it was his turn to step into his father's shoes and run for office. In June of 1941 Joe Jr. decides to enlist, he begins training as a naval officer Jack also joins the navy but his medical problems made it difficult. Jack commands a PT boat in the South Pacific. On the night of August 1, 1943 a Japanese destroyer cuts his boat in half but Jack rounded up all his crew members and swam to the nearest island where there was no Japanese bombers four hours away. Jack returned home a war hero and was praised for his courage and hard work making both Joe and Rose very proud. With Jack a war hero Joe Jr. feels under new pressure to prove his own courage for his political career Joe volunteers for a dangerous bombing mission in France making it fearful for his parents and Jack. Jack tried talking Joe out of it, but he was determined to complete the mission. Joe's plane takes off filled with explosives and the plane explodes in midair on August 12, 1944 Joe Jr. is dead at the age of 29 his body is never recovered. It was a hard loss for Joe and Rose and Kennedy's siblings and mostly hard for Jack. Joe was mad and believed God let him die. He told his wife Rose he was never praying again to the cross she prays to all the time. With Jack leaving the navy with his health issues and with Joe Jr. dead he is now the focus of his father's political ambitions. John Kennedy wastes no time entering politics he runs for Congress in 1946 Joe Kennedy has the political background and wealth to make it happen and Jack wins by a landslide. Soon after Kennedy takes office another tragedy soon follows in May of 1948 Jacks sister Kathleen is killed in a plane crash, Jack was devastated he just had a sense that life was really unfair. Life is short he would say, you have to live everyday like it's your last day on Earth. On September 12, 1953 John Kennedy married Jacqueline "Jackie" Bouvier they were married after he was elected United States Senator of Massachusetts. Their second child Caroline was born in 1957 and is now the only surviving child of John and Jackie's children. John F. Kennedy Jr. known as John-John was born in late November 1960 after his father was elected the 35th President of the United States. JFK Jr. was killed in a plane crash in July of 1999 near Martha's Vineyard along with his wife and sister-in-law. Jackie had suffered a miscarriage in 1955 and a stillbirth in 1956 and a son Patrick Bouvier Kennedy who died two days after birth in August of 1963. John Kennedy faced a lot of his own problems with his health and back problems and problems during his presidency. Kennedy once said, "If the country knew what shape I was in they would boot me out of here." Kennedy's father Joseph Kennedy had suffered a massive stroke on December 19, 1961 and it left him paralyzed on his left side and he was unable to speak, Joe spent the rest of his life in a wheelchair. He remained at his home in Hyannis Port where the Kennedy family came to visit. The Kennedy's always went to Hyannis Port for every holiday to spend it with Joe and Rose. It was fun for all the kids to get together and John Kennedy would take them on golf cart rides in the front yard. They were all about family and spent many times all together at the Cape. It was a time for John and the rest of the Kennedy children to spend time with their father Joseph Kennedy. In November 1963 the week before Thanksgiving Joe Kennedy's second son President Kennedy was shot and killed while making a political trip to Dallas, Texas. Lyndon Johnson was sworn in as the 36th President of the United States before Air Force One left for Washington with Jackie Kennedy and the body and remains of his former Chief Executive. Mrs. Rose Kennedy spoke with Johnson briefly on Air Force One as he gave his condolences to her and

Joe Kennedy for the loss of their son. Johnson wanted justice to be done, he thought that this could have been an international communist conspiracy but unfortunately wasn't successful after a second bullet killed the alleged presidential assassin. Nine months into Johnson's presidency Bobby Kennedy resigns as Attorney General and decides to stay at home with his wife and all his children. Kennedy spent a lot of time with Jackie, Caroline and John-John after Jack was killed in Dallas. It had been told that he and Jackie had their own affair after Jack's death and that Jackie leaned on Bobby Kennedy for a lot. In 1968 Bobby took the Democratic seat for the Presidency, he campaigned to carry on what his brother John started, that ended with his assassination at the Ambassador Hotel in Los Angeles, California. Kennedy died early the next morning due to his gunshot wounds. Ethel Kennedy gave birth to her last child Rory Kennedy in December of 1968 six months after Bobby's death. She became a documentary film maker and interviewed her mother about what kind of a person her father was. By 1969 Joe and Rose Kennedy outlived four of their nine children. Joe Kennedy died at his home in Hyannis Port on November 18, 1969. Jackie Kennedy and the kids moved to

Grease when she married Greek shipping man Aristotle Onassis in 1968 he kept her and her children safe away from the United States Jackie Kennedy feared for her children lives there after both Jack and Bobby were killed. In 1973 Onassis's son Alexander was killed in a plane crash after he died Onassis's health started to go downhill. He died of respiratory failure at the age of 69 in Paris of March 1975. Jackie eventually accepted $26 million dollars from Christina Onassis, Aristotle's daughter. Jackie and the children moved to New York where Jackie became a publisher for a short time but stopped after her boss gave the okay to publish a book that talked about assassinating Ted Kennedy the last brother. Jackie Kennedy Onassis became sick in November of 1993 when she was diagnosed with lymphoma. By March of 1994 the cancer had spread to her spinal cord and brain. Mrs. Onassis died in her sleep at her home in New York at the age of 64 on May 18, 1994. Ted Kennedy was the last living brother of the family and was always there for Jackie after Jack and Bobby died. He was always there for her to lean on and spend time with he was one of the first people Jackie told that she was diagnosed with cancer. Kennedy won United States Senator in 1962 in the summer of 1969 he almost put that career and his own life at risk. On July 18, 1969 Ted Kennedy attended a party on Chappaquiddick Island, off the east coast of Martha's Vineyard, Massachusetts. It was a celebration in honor of the dedicated work of the Boiler Room Girls and was the fourth such reunion of Robert F. Kennedy campaign workers. Ted reportedly left the party at 11:15 p.m. with Mary Jo Kopechne one of Bobby's political campaign members. They didn't tell anyone that they were leaving Kennedy was apparently taking Kopechne to catch the last ferry back to Edgartown, where she was staying. Kennedy drove his 1967 Oldsmobile Delmont off a narrow bridge, the car landed on its roof in Poucha Pond. Kennedy was able to escape from the vehicle and survived, but Kopechne did not. She died in the submerged car, eight days before her 29th birthday. Ted Kennedy failed to report the accident to authorities until the car and Kopechne's body was discovered the next morning. Mary Jo's parents found out that their daughter died directly from Kennedy the next morning before he informed authorities. Kennedy under the influence of alcohol put the family to shame. Her parents later on found out from wire press releases later on that Kennedy was the driver. A week after the incident

Kennedy pleaded guilty to leaving the scene of an accident and was given a suspended sentence of two months in jail. He remained as U.S Senator from Massachusetts for 47 years and was known as the lion of the senate. Kennedy died of brain cancer on August 25, 2009 he was diagnosed nine months before his death. For many people of this country the name Kennedy is something that everyone talks about dating back to the 1930's and on. They were a political family who had dreams for themselves and their country, dreams that could change the world and make it a better place. With their political knowledge and ideas they made those dreams come true for all people. Joe Kennedy had many affairs or more during his marriage like Jack did. Joe brought home an eighteen year old girl right in front of Rose while they had company and would bring the girl upstairs like it was nothing. It didn't bother him that his wife was there. His actions led his sons to fool around with women behind their wives. John Kennedy fooled around with big names like Marilyn Monroe, Judith Campbell and other women who were connected to the mafia that Bobby Kennedy was investigating for organized crime. FBI director J. Edgar Hoover challenged the president by warning him that his private life had now become a matter of public interest. JFK started seeing Monroe after he was warned about Judith Campbell. In the eyes of J. Edgar Hoover Marilyn Monroe was just as dangerous as Judith Campbell. With JFK having affairs during his presidency it was hard for the Kennedy administration at keeping it quiet and for his wife who was in the same house as him while he was doing these acts. As most people say Kennedy was addicted to sex. It was a Kennedy thing with Joe Kennedy and the brothers. Is there a Kennedy curse? Why?

Chapter 7

A Tragic End to a Great Man

John F. Kennedy was a busy man, his work never stopped in Washington, Hyannis Port, and Palm Beach Florida. He saw the future and what it held, he promised the country he would keep us out of war and he did. Kennedy told us we would put a man on the moon before the decade was over, even though he wasn't here to see it happen, it did in 1969 with the whole country watching. When John Kennedy was on television people would stop all around the nation and watch as he spoke. He spoke from his heart and spoke with courage in his words and passion in his eyes; he kept the country at ease during both its good and bad times. As he said in his inaugural address on January 20, 1961 "the torch has been passed to a new generation of Americans." After succeeding President Eisenhower one of our countries older president's to hold office. The citizens of our nation saw a promising future that would help their children and their grandchildren, it was the beginning of a new era. Though Kennedy wasn't always at ease and relaxed as the president, he had it like every other former Chief Executive, keeping the country out of war, helping the south with discrimination, talking to the nation on live television, and more. President Kennedy never showed that he was scared, he came up with an idea and he would do it quick, making sure that every citizen was safe and that they knew where our country stood. Kennedy knew how to get the public's attention, and that was his children he knew he could catch the nation's eye with pictures of Caroline and John Jr. when Jackie was away he had his secretary go get the kids and have his photographer take pictures of the kids playing and dancing around in the oval office with him. When the pictures got out of course the people loved them and JFK thought it was awesome. They were one of the most admired first families ever, they were the first family we all knew by first name. In 1961 it was Mrs. Kennedy who discovered the resolute desk was stored away in a closet and she demanded that it would come out for the president to use for his term. It was a gift given to President Hayes by Queen Victoria. President and Mrs. Kennedy brought class and charm to the White House and made sure it looked perfect for every public event. Though Mrs. Kennedy did not have it easy either in the White House because of

Jack's womanizing she kept her emotions to herself and left some times to go to Virginia with the kids and Nanny Shaw. Jack had a women problem as his brother Bobby would tell him. Most people say it's a Kennedy thing Jack's father Joe was the same way along with his brothers but the Kennedy's were Irish Catholics and divorce was not accepted in the church. Jack didn't see the problem with seeing other women, which was what he was taught by Joe Kennedy himself. Jacks behavior soon changed in 1963 when his wife was pregnant with their third child. With JFK still at the White House taking care of things a phone call was made to him in the summer of 1963 that Mrs. Kennedy went into labor. It was a boy Patrick Bouvier Kennedy but Patrick's lungs were not fully developed yet and he was put in an incubator to help them develop. Just two days after birth Patrick died. John and Jackie became closer after the death of their son Patrick and Jack changed to be the man his wife deserved. JFK was ready to get on the campaign trail again and asked Jackie to help him get re-elected in the 1964 election. Jackie agreed to travel with Jack, he had his mind set on Texas he was afraid he was going to lose it in 1964 and he needed Texas to win. The trip began in San Antonio for a two day five speech tour of the lone star state. On the morning of November 22, 1963 it couldn't have been a better day the sun was out the crowds were big and eager to see their President. President Kennedy began his morning at a breakfast at his hotel in Fort Worth he arrived early and all the crowd cheered for was Jackie they wanted to see their first lady of the United States. Jackie Kennedy who was still in a daze from losing her son Patrick three months before had a hard time getting ready, President Kennedy wanted her to come down for the breakfast and join him and the crowd. When all was quiet Jackie Kennedy made her way into the hall dressed in her stunning pink gown and hat with her beautiful white gloves covering her hands, she smiled as she got to her table and President Kennedy began his speech. JFK joked that he was the man who accompanied Mrs. Kennedy to Paris and he had some of that same sensation as he travel Texas. Jack also joked that no one ever wondered what he and Lyndon Johnson wear, the crowd broke out in laughter. What John and Jackie both didn't know was Jack was not going to make it back home to Washington alive. After Fort Worth was over Kennedy was ready to take on Dallas and it was a bright day which meant he wanted the bubbletop down on his motorcade which put the secret service agent's nerves on edge. Kennedy used to tell everyone "I couldn't get elected dog catcher if I didn't go out into the crowd and greet the people." And everyone loved it, they were so excited to shake hands with their president. John and Jackie arrived in Dallas about 11:30 that morning with Governor Connolly and his wife Nellie and Vice President Johnson and Mrs. Johnson, Mrs. Kennedy was greeted with beautiful red roses she followed Jack into the crowd where he went to shake hands with people at the gate, secret service watched closely. The President made it clear to them that they were to ride in the follow-up car behind them and not with him in his motorcade. Kennedy did not want the public to think that he was scared or that he had something against the public. The crowds were huge and got bigger as the motorcade made its way down Main Street, with the sun shining, the big crowds, and The President and his glamorous wife making their way through Dallas it was a day that everyone in Dallas will remember especially when the car took the turn onto Elm Street. It was a moment that changed everything for secret service, our country, and the Kennedy Administration. Mrs. Kennedy held her husband until they arrived at Parkland Memorial Hospital. Then got him onto a stretcher and quickly wheeled him to trauma room one. Agents and Mrs. Kennedy stared at the commander and chief as he laid there badly wounded. It was something no one in that hospital could wrap their head around. Not even doctors and nurses, they cleared everyone out to be ready for President Kennedy. Why did it happen? Mrs. Kennedy sat outside trauma room one soaked with the president's blood and brain matter stuck to her jewelry and clothes. The doctors tried everything possible to save their beloved president the secret service however knew it was over. Kennedy had requested a priest come to give the president last rights. Seeing that the Kennedy's were big Catholics. Father Oscar Hubert was sent to the hospital to give President Kennedy last rights of the Catholic Church, Mr. Kennedy was wrapped in a sheet and placed in a casket from the Oneal Funeral home that Mrs. Kennedy's secret service agent Clint Hill called for. That afternoon Air Force One left Texas with a new President. Back in Washington at Bethesda Naval Hospital where President Kennedy's autopsy was done Mrs. Kennedy, Robert Kennedy and some of her staff waited for the president's body to be done. Mrs. Kennedy thought it was appropriate that his autopsy be done at Bethesda Naval hospital because her husband was a naval officer. President John Kennedy left a legacy that is hard to forget. He was a living legend and America was shocked and devastated losing their beloved Chief Executive. In an interview after the Kennedy assassination Jackie Kennedy said to the reporter that she walked behind her husband's casket hoping someone in the crowd would take a shot at her and kill her so she can be with Jack. That shows how much Jack meant to her despite their ups and downs throughout their marriage. I think many Americans believe it was just hard after seeing Jack be murdered. In the end after losing their son Patrick they became closer and were both finally happy. 2 months later Mrs. Kennedy not only buried her son, but she also had to bury her husband and father of their two young children. President Kennedy was in office for 1,000 days, he was hoping for re-election in 1964 along with the rest of the country. Mrs. Kennedy suffered from PTSD after Jack's assassination. It was a living nightmare on that faithful day in Dallas. It was the shot heard around the world and along with the passing of our 35th president so to pass the hopes and dreams of young Americans who lived through the 1,000 day

Presidency know as Camelot.

Chapter 8

The Warren Commission

We all know what happened on November 22, 1963, but do we really know how it happened? A week after the Kennedy Assassination President Lyndon Johnson put together the Warren Commission headed by Chief of Justice Earl Warren. But the question is... Was the Warren Commission right? The Warren Commission concluded that Lee Harvey Oswald fired the shots that killed John F. Kennedy from the 6th floor of the Texas School Book Depository and he acted alone in doing it. They also concluded that Jack Ruby acted alone in killing Oswald. Five decades later there are many different opinions about what took place on that day in Dealey Plaza. Lee Harvey Oswald was on the 6th floor of the Book Depository and did have his rifle with him that day at work. Oswald did have a bird's eye view of Dealey Plaza anyone could have made that shot. The last shot which was the fatal shot that blew the president's head off is questionable. Could Oswald make that last shot? According to the Warren Commission he did fire all three shots. The public however since November 22, 1963 have had other thoughts and believe Oswald did not act alone. Many believe there was a conspiracy and others were involved. . The Warren Commission said there was no evidence that told them there was a conspiracy and they completely ignored the Zapruder film and other evidence that could have helped them find out about John Kennedy's assassination. The Warren Commission also concluded that the second shot that hit Kennedy in the back of his neck also hit Governor Connolly and the condition of the bullet was perfect. This is called The One Bullet Two Victim Theory. What the Warren Commission claims is that the second bullet hit Kennedy in the back of his neck exited through his throat continued on and hit Governor Connolly in his back, came out of his chest, hit his hand and landed in is leg. That perfectly intact bullet did all of that. Putting yourself in Oswald's position on that day in Dealey Plaza was quite simple. He had the perfect view for any possible assassination. After the 2nd gunshot when the motorcade got closer to the underpass that 3rd shot captured in the Zapruder film shows Kennedy's head being thrown towards the left and back. That can indicate a few things. There could have possibly been a man behind the grassy knoll who fired that third and fatal shot. Some people there said they heard a shot come from the grassy knoll area. President Kennedy's motorcade was going slow at 5 mph so the crowd can get a good look at their president, when the last shot was fired it seemed that the motorcade had sped up making it look like that fatal shot just hit Kennedy as the motorcade started to go faster causing his head to be thrown to the left and rear. It can mean it came from the front or somewhere close to the book depository. There is so much evidence that the Warren Commission completely ignored. Oswald a former Marine knew how to handle a rifle, he certainly had some experience and Dallas police were almost certain this was their guy that shot the president. Kennedy was very well liked however, in Dallas that morning Jackie mentioned to him about the papers going around that said Kennedy wanted for Treason. President Kennedy reply to his wife by saying, "Yes, we are heading into nut country today." The Warren Commission had a lot of evidence to look at for their conclusion and the evidence of Jack Ruby sneaking into the basement of the Dallas city jail with a gun with everyone not knowing he would do that. Oswald's death is what led most of us to believe Kennedy's assassination resulted in nothing other than a conspiracy. Plus the fact

he had been seen in the jail walking around since

November 22nd when Oswald was taken into custody

should be most of the evidence they needed for this case.

In Washington September 6, 1978 a committee of the

House of Representatives began public hearings in the

assassination in 1963 of John F. Kennedy. There was

expert testimonies about the autopsy, the murder

weapon, and the direction of which the shots came.

Committee sources didn't expect them to solve all the

mysteries about the Kennedy assassination but the

committee did expect its scientific evidence to settle once

and for all whether there was a single assassin or whether

there was another gunman there that day in Dealey Plaza.

At the moment of the headshot we see the president

thrown to the rear and to his left which would seemly

indicate a shot from the right front of the area of the

grassy knoll. The committee experts agree that one bullet

enter President Kennedy's back and exited through his

throat. There is also other agreements that the fatal shot

entered the back of his head and came out the front. But

committee experts are not sure on another key question

could a single 3 inch bullet go through President Kennedy's

back and neck then smash through Governor Connolly's back, wrist, and thigh... The Warren Commission said yes. 25 years after John F. Kennedy was killed in Dallas the mystery of his assassination and the fascination of that mystery both remained strong. There was a CBS News Times Poll taking in October of 1988 that said 2/3 of Americans did not believe Lee Harvey Oswald acted alone and only 13% thought he did. And more than 60% believe there was an official cover-up to keep the public from learning the truth. Almost 6 decades after the most shattering murder of our time. The case is still not closed. It is awful that the public can't and probably will never know the truth about the Kennedy assassination mostly the public who lived it and saw it. And watched it on television for 4 days straight 24/7. Another issue brought up after the assassination was the man standing by the grassy knoll on a hot sunny day with an umbrella. He opened his umbrella when the shots were fired. This made investigators think that he was signaling someone to fire the shots. As the shots rang out the man opened his umbrella and when President Kennedy went through the triple underpass the man closed his umbrella and while other people were running and dropping to the ground he just stood there. I think that there are two issues being raised here one is what he was doing during the assassination. And two would be what he was doing admittedly following the assassination. The House Select Committees had evidence that the umbrella didn't contain a gun or weapon of any kind during the assassination but it is very concerning why that man was there with an umbrella when John Kennedy was shot and why he had an umbrella on a warm and sunny day. Although it was concluded that the umbrella man was not involved or had a weapon in his umbrella that day it is to this day suspicious of what he did. Whether the Warren Commission believed there was a conspiracy or not there was still a lot they had to investigate. The shot that killed Oswald tells the whole thing. That made most people realize that the Kennedy assassination was a planned conspiracy. Not only was Jack Ruby connected to the Mafia but so was John Kennedy and his father ambassador Joe Kennedy, Frank Sinatra (John's friend), and his younger brother attorney general Robert Kennedy who started the organized crime which made the mob mad to begin with during the Kennedy administration. If Lee Harvey Oswald acted alone, then why would Jack Ruby just decide out of nowhere to go down to the Dallas city jail to kill Oswald on the morning of his transfer? Lee Harvey Oswald was a suspected suspect and had enough evidence behind the Kennedy assassination. Oswald had a perfect view at the Book Depository where he worked on Elm Street of the President's route. He had an even better view of the president making his turn from Houston Street onto Elm. It was a perfect shot when the motorcade slowed down to almost 5 mph to make a sharp turn onto Elm. When the first shot was fired Governor Connolly turns to look over his left shoulder he didn't see anything, he then was in the process of looking over his right shoulder when he felt a blow hit him in the back as if someone had hit him with a doubled up fist. The force was so strong it bent him over and as he looked down he immediately saw he was covered in blood. In the Zapruder Film it shows President Kennedy and Governor Connolly reacting almost at the same time. The confusion for many investigators was the condition of the bullet what many call the pristine bullet because of how perfectly in tacked it was after hitting both men. There was a total of nine wounds four to President Kennedy and five to Governor Connolly. The Warren Commission simply ignored all this information, the

Zapruder film, the grassy knoll and conspiracy theories. In response of Ruby's killing of Oswald, the Warren Commission declared that the news media had responsibility with the Dallas police department for "law enforcement." That led to Lee Oswald's death. In other words instead of looking into all the evidence that was given to the Warren Commission they blamed the media and Dallas police for the murder of Lee Oswald. The Warren Commission concluded that pressure of the press, radio, and television networks for Oswald's information about the prison transfer resulted in lax security pressures for Lee Oswald in the basement of the city jail allowing Jack Ruby to enter when no one noticed because of the security and news men all around making Ruby fit in and get a spot where he patiently waited to shoot and kill President Kennedy's accused assassin. Ruby knew almost every officer in Dallas most of them went to his bar and strip club the Carousel Club in downtown Dallas. The officers there who noticed Ruby probably didn't think Ruby was going to kill their suspected assassin. The Warren Commissions purpose was to at least try and solve some of the answers about the Kennedy assassination although they believed and confirmed that Lee Harvey

Oswald killed John F. Kennedy and that he acted alone in doing it, they raised more questions for the American people. Not only questions about why Oswald killed John Kennedy, but why Jack Ruby killed Lee Oswald. Many of us believe that there were others involved. Oswald while being taken into custody claimed he was a patsy and denied everything Dallas Police asked him. The Warren Commission had many facts about Oswald that Dallas police found out within the 48 hours they had Oswald in custody. Lee Oswald was the chairman of a fair play for the Cuba Committee Oswald supported Cuba because it was the only country that supported Marxism. September 27, 1963 Oswald went to the Cuban Embassy to ask to move to Cuba and get his citizenship there for his support for President Castro. He was denied and sent back home. Oswald had purchased a hand gun and rifle in March of 1963 under the name A. J. Hidell. Oswald made the name up with his picture on the identification card. The Warren Commission found nothing suspicious of these acts Oswald made in 1963 along with the killing of him just two days after Kennedy was murdered. Oswald's support for Cuba was a red flag from the beginning considering the United States and Cuba almost went to war during the Cuban

Missile Crisis in October of 1962. Jack Ruby was a well-known man with many connections, Mafia connections. Ruby was friends with the mob. There is no doubt the mob hated the Kennedy's the big question was how Jack Ruby got into the picture. Was he hired by the mob? If Oswald lived and had gone on trial there would be more answers about others being involved with Lee Oswald and if there was more than one shooter. With Ruby shooting Oswald and killing him 48 hours after President Kennedy was assassinated right before Oswald even can stand trial is a mystery. What Jack Ruby did has not solved the assassination of John F. Kennedy, but gave one clue. It had to have been a planned conspiracy. The Warren Commission wanted nothing to do with the evidence of a conspiracy. Lee Harvey Oswald fits for a patsy, he looks guilty not just for the Kennedy assassination but for anything. The Warren Commission did one thing. They told the public what they wanted to hear.

Chapter 9

The Secret Service Detail

The Secret Service has one job and that is to protect the most powerful person in the country. It may seem simple but it is a big job no matter how many people there are to protect the president. Back in 1963 there used to be 5 to 7 agents around the president and that was the secret service. Kennedy had great secret service agents, they became family and he was always so generous to them and was grateful for all they did for him, Mrs. Kennedy, and the kids. The secret service doesn't only have the job of protecting the President but also the first family. The Kennedy detail was always on top of President Kennedy and watched every move he made. President Kennedy always wanted to shake hands with the public every chance he got and wanted to talk to anyone he can possibly talk to. He knew how to get elected and re-elected and that was to be in the public spot light which made the egg shells even thinner for the secret service whose job was to guard the man. In November of 1963 Kennedy was ready to campaign for the 1964 presidential election. It was to be a 2 day five speech tour of the state of Texas. In Dallas the secret service requested the bubble top on the president's motorcade be up for the journey through Dallas, but President Kennedy made it clear he will only use the top if it was raining out. If the sun was out that day the top must be down, he wanted the public to be able to see their president. The secret service agents were worried, they were so worried about the president riding in an open limo. The agents were in charge of protecting the president and they didn't like the fact that President Kennedy wanted to ride in an open car. But the president loved open limos. He wanted the world to see that there was nothing bad between him and his citizens. It was a huge event for President Kennedy and the citizens of Dallas but also a security nightmare for Clint Hill and the rest of the secret service. The motorcade moved slowly, they made their way through Downtown Dallas. Clint Hill was a former secret service agent assigned to Mrs. Kennedy. He is also the bodyguard climbing on the back of the motorcade in Dallas. Years on he still hasn't forgiven himself for not saving the President's life. He saw the president grab at his throat and moved quickly to his left and he knew something was wrong. So he jumped from the follow-up car and ran to the president's motorcade to guard him and Mrs. Kennedy. Just as he got to the car the third shot rang out and it hit the president in the head making a small explosion. Clint Hill got on the car where Mrs. Kennedy was on the trunk grabbing a piece of the presidents skull that had blown off. When he got on the car the president's body fell into Mrs. Kennedy's lap and he considered it a fatal wound so he turned around and gave a thumbs down to the other agents in the follow-up car. At Parkland Hospital Mrs. Kennedy didn't want anyone to see the President so Hill took off his jacket and covered the president's head and upper chest and she let them take him in the hospital. When they got inside Clint Hill phones Washington to let them know what is going on while he was talking the phone was interrupted by the attorney general the President's brother. Bobby asked him what's going on down there because he didn't really know so he explained it to him. And then Bobby said, "Well how bad is it." Hill did not want to tell him that his brother was dead so he simply said well it's as bad as it can get. Then at 1:00 Dallas time the doctors came out and said the president has died. The president is dead. Clint had called for a casket and they loaded him in a casket. When Secret

Service Agent Paul Landis arrived at Dallas Love Field he went up to agent Winston Lawson and asked him if he was assigned to the follow-up car with the other agents. And he was with the other agents riding behind the president's motorcade. He said the trip was really going well. But when they hit Main Street the crowds really started to get bigger and were moving into the road which made him and the other agents very nervous. Coming to the end of Main and turning onto Houston Street the crowds got a lot smaller. Then the car took a left onto Elm Street which put them right in front of the Texas School Book Depository. When they got further down Elm Street Paul heard a sound come from over his right shoulder he admittedly identified it as a gunshot he was a hunter, he fired high powered rifles, and he knew what the sound was. He then saw agent Clint Hill jump from the car and ran to the motorcade and all he kept saying was come on Clint go, go, go. And then he heard a another shot and it sounded like it hit something hollow like a melon and he saw the President's head explode and Paul knew he wasn't going to survive. Winston Lawson arrived at Dallas Love Field at 9:30 a.m. he was assigned to the follow-up car. President Kennedy and Jackie arrived around 11:30 a.m. Lawson rode in the follow-up car next to Paul Landis behind the president's motorcade. When the car turned onto Elm Street he remembers hearing 3 shots. He said many people were confused where the shots came from he said he didn't hear a shot come from in front of him or a shot come from the side of him he said that 3rd shot came from behind me at the Texas Book Depository back over his right shoulder. He described the seen on Elm Street and all he heard was bang... bang.... bang. At Parkland he was standing by the president's head where it was bleeding profusely. He didn't leave the president until he was in the casket. Lawson claims no one will ever change his mind that last shot came from directly behind him back at the Book Depository. During the assassination of President Kennedy Dave Powers and Kenny O'Donnell his political aids were riding in the secret service car behind the president. Dave Powers said, "I saw his hand waving and now he puts his hand slowly to his throat and slumps toward Jackie and I say to Kenny I think the president has been hit. Kenny and I not only saw the next one we heard it, we just saw that handsome head get blown off." They heard the shot and they heard the impact of the shot. Powers said it was the most sickening thing "like a grapefruit thrown against a brick wall." When they got to Parkland Hospital Kenny O'Donnell can't go close he can't look at him but Dave Powers goes running up. Dave Powers: "At Parkland I ran up to the presidential car his eyes were open I opened the door and said Oh my God Mr. President and I almost expected him to say I'm alright because he never complained." A fragment of the bullet came out of President Kennedy's forehead while Dave was standing there. He called for a stretcher and helped the other agents get President Kennedy inside Parkland Hospital. Clint Hill along with agents Kellerman Greer and Rufus Youngblood provided testimony to the Warren Commission in Washington D.C on March 9, 1964. The Warren Commission stated how there were no agents on the back of the motorcade. The president had told the agents multiple times during the Florida trip and the Dallas trip he didn't want them on the back of the motorcade unless it was very necessary. The sun was out so the bubble top was down and the agents couldn't do anything but respect the president's wishes to stay off the back of the motorcade. Hill got to the car 2 seconds after the fatal shot was fired. When the 3rd shot hit Kennedy in the head the driver accelerated the car causing Hill to slip away from the car. Hill knew that the president was dead. He and all the other agents didn't leave the president's side in the trauma room. When doctors found Kennedy still had a heartbeat the agents watch as they desperately tried to save the president's life. The motorcade had blood everywhere, Mrs. Kennedy was covered in blood. There was so much blood no one can tell if there was any other wounds to President Kennedy other than a huge gaping wound in the right portion of the head. Nurses asked the agents to wait in the hallway with everyone else, but they refused. Their job was to stay with the president at all times, they didn't leave President Kennedy. Doctors and nurses had no choice but to work on Kennedy with the agents in the trauma room. Hill and the other agents knew Kennedy was dead so they had called for a priest to come give Kennedy last rights. At 1:00 p.m. when the president was officially pronounced dead Clint Hill calls for a casket. The agents fought local law enforcers to take Kennedy's body back to Washington the nation's Capital where the autopsy will be done there. Back at Love field the agents carry their president they had sworn to protect onto Air Force One. The casket wouldn't fit through the door so the agents had to take the handles off the casket to get it inside the plane. They got the casket and Mrs. Kennedy settled then the agents watched as a new president was sworn in. Back at Washington D.C cameras and news stations gathered at Andrew's air force base to get a glimpse of the casket being brought down the plane carrying the body and remains of President Kennedy. A Marine honor guard awaited for President Kennedy's casket to arrive to be brought for the autopsy but the agents wanted to carry the casket to the ambulance as they served their commander and chief one last time. It was after 4 in the morning on November 23rd and the agents were all tired they had been up since early morning the day before which what they thought would be a normal day. The next day on Saturday November 23, 1963 Mrs. Kennedy and Bobby Kennedy the president's brother wanted to look at him one last time. Clint Hill stepped back as they stood by the open casket. Mrs. Kennedy then called for Mr. Hill asking him for a pair of scissors. Clint Hill brought Mrs. Kennedy the scissors then when he walked away he heard the scissors go clip, clip. He assumed Mrs. Kennedy had taken a lock of the President's hair. Although the Kennedy detail was stunned at their failure to protect President Kennedy, everyone agreed Clint Hills fast and brave actions was truly courageous. Clint Hill was honored at a ceremony in Washington days after President Kennedy's funeral. Mrs. Kennedy despite being in mourning of her husband's shocking death made an appearance at the event to thank Mr. Hill in person for his heroic actions on that tragic day in Dealey Plaza. Clint Hill stayed assigned to Mrs. Kennedy and Caroline and John Jr. until after the 1964 presidential election. He was then assigned to President Johnson, Nixon, and Ford before retiring from the service. No secret service detail has been through horror protecting the President of the United States than President Kennedy's secret service agents. It was the moment that changed everything for their country, their professions and themselves.

Chapter 10
The Patsy

A patsy... That's what Oswald told reporters he was. Why wouldn't Oswald explain more about him being a "patsy?" Why was he a patsy? Who else was in on the Kennedy assassination with him? About a month before President Kennedy's arrival in Texas, Lee Harvey Oswald gets a job as a clerk at the Texas School Book Depository on the corner of Houston and Elm Street in Dallas, Texas. It was a dull looking six-story building. Oswald had a hard time looking for work after moving from New Orleans to Texas. He wasn't living with his wife and was being watched by the FBI. The morning of November 22, 1963 Oswald arrives at work with a long paper package that he claimed carried curtain rods. Could this be the package that contained the rifle found on the 6th floor? When Oswald leaves work without telling anyone his absence creates a stir, and police broadcast his description over the radios. Did he have it planned to bring a rifle to work? If Oswald said he was curtain rods then where were these curtain rods he was talking about. The police mainly focused on the Book

Depository and the details that were coming in about the suspect they believe was behind the assassination. Oswald reportedly goes back home changes his jacket and takes his 38 revolver with him, killed a police officer with it and then fled the scene and hid inside the Texas Theater. Did Oswald have plan to shoot the officer? Was he scared the officer would take him to the Dallas jail if he talked to him? Dallas Police arrived and surrounded the Texas Theater people gathered outside to get a glimpse of police arresting Kennedy's assassin. Police scatter into the movie theater Oswald is seated near the back as police surround Oswald and an officer yells, "On your feet!" Oswald is then caught and brought to Dallas Police Headquarters. Oswald is pulled out of the Texas Theater kicking and screaming. He is put into a police cruiser and taken to the Dallas city jail. He is brought into custody where he was about to have his first interrogation. Officer Gus Rose and Richard S. Stovall questioned Lee Harvey Oswald when Dallas police brought him to the Dallas City Jail. They brought Oswald in and Gus Rose said, "Who is this?" and they told him they have the man who shot Officer Tippit and he matches the suspect who killed President Kennedy. So Officer Rose took the handcuffs off Oswald making him feel more comfortable. He figured Oswald would open up and talk without being handcuffed to the chair. Officer Rose asked him what his name was and he refused to tell him so he searched him and in his pocket was a wallet and in the wallet was two pieces of identification one card said Lee H. Oswald and the other card said Alex J. Hidell when Rose asked him who these people were or which one of these he was Oswald said, "well you're the cop you figure it out." So Officer Rose and a couple other officers went to ask Oswald's wife Marina questions when he got to the house Marina said, "Come in I have been expecting you." Rose explained to her what was going on and asked her if her husband owned a gun and she said yes and he said can you show me where it is and she said yes and she motioned him to follow her to a door in the kitchen which led to a garage. She pointed out a blanket to them and said the gun was wrapped up in the blanket. So they picked it up and there was nothing in the blanket, the rifle was gone. Marina's heart sunk, all she thought was oh no, was Lee involved in this. The reason it was so clear to her that Lee did it or was involved was when they mentioned the shots came from the building where he worked. Oswald owned guns and knew how to operate them being a former ex-marine. He claimed the brown paper bag he brought into work that day was curtain rods he had to take back home to his house. After the assassination when police officers surround the Texas School Book Depository and go inside to investigate the situation up on the sixth floor was a snipers perch, 3 bullet cartridges, and a 30 caliber rifle in the far corner of the sixth floor. Captain Will Fritz took a head count of all employees at the book depository and they had one employee missing who happened to be Oswald and that was a red flag to all law enforcement officers at that moment. Why did Oswald leave without telling anyone? Why didn't they ask where the curtain rods were? Again Oswald denies killing President Kennedy from the Book Depository. Was this a plan or a conspiracy? All of the evidence that the Dallas Police has about Oswald he denies. He tells police he has no idea who Alex Hidell is and why he has that identification card. Now why would Lee Harvey Oswald have this identification card with his picture and a different name and not know why he was carrying it? Police show Oswald the picture that Marina had brought down to Dallas Police headquarters of Oswald standing in his backyard in their other house back in New Orleans of him standing there holding the rifle they found in the book depository and his handgun in his right pant pocket that he had on him in the Texas Theater. Captain Fritz asked Oswald when that picture was taken and he claims he has no idea who the person is in that picture. Everyone in the interrogation room stopped. Captain Fritz basically said, "So this is not you in the picture?" Oswald told him no it was his face put on another person's body from another picture. At that point Fritz had enough of Oswald. He just kept on denying every piece of evidence they had against him. Why does Oswald deny all this? Is he covering for someone else? Oswald looked at a picture of himself his wife took back at their home in New Orleans and told police that it wasn't him in the picture. That is suspicious. Dallas police are almost certain that this is the man who murdered John F. Kennedy and very certain he also killed Officer Tippit as well. After Oswald told police he didn't know anything about the picture of him or his fake ID, Dallas police had enough of him. Oswald who defected to the Soviet Union always wanted to become a citizen of Cuba. Oswald went to the Cuban Embassy in Mexico City for his citizenship in support of President Castro. Oswald was denied and sent back home. Oswald was told by a

Cuban consular officer that he was disinclined to approve the visa, saying "a person like Oswald in place of aiding the Cuban Revolution, was doing it harm. Is Oswald's support of Cuba and President Castro the reason he may have been involved in Kennedy's murder? President Kennedy ended all problems with Cuba and Castro in 1962 after the country almost went to war during the Cuban Missile Crisis. Was the "patsy" working for President Castro? FBI agents visited Oswald's wife's house where she was living with her friend Ruth Paine and her two young daughters a couple of weeks before November 22nd. They went there twice to speak to her about Lee. About 2 to 3 weeks before Kennedy's assassination Oswald was looking for FBI Agent James Hosty. He was a special agent assigned to Oswald since his return from the Soviet Union. He left Hosty a note on his desk saying he was going to blow up the FBI office and Dallas Police Department if Hosty kept bothering his wife Marina. He told Hosty if he has something to say about him to ask him up front and leave his wife out of it. Hosty destroyed Oswald's note after Oswald was named the suspect in the Kennedy assassination. In the days prior to Kennedy's arrival to Dallas, local newspapers published the route of the

Presidential Motorcade, which happened to pass by the book depository where Oswald worked. Did that give him the idea to kill Kennedy? Oswald doesn't admit to anything and denies, denies, denies. Police Chief Jesse Curry wants Lee Oswald to be transferred to the Dallas county jail where he felt it was more secure for their prisoner. He made plan for Oswald to be transferred on Sunday morning November 24, 1963. Curry said to the press that precautions will be taken of course and Oswald will be transferred in an armored car that morning from city jail to county jail. The day before Oswald is taken from room to room in the Dallas City Jail to be questioned by different people. While he is being taken all over the jail he has to walk by all the newsmen in the hallway of the jail who were there with cameras asking Oswald a lot of questions. Oswald answers to one of the reporters: "I'm just a patsy." We don't know why Oswald was a patsy. On the morning of November 24, 1963 Lee Harvey Oswald is taken to Captain Fritz's office for one last interrogation before the transfer. Fritz stuck with the same questions he had along. "Lee did you shoot the president?" and Oswald would respond "no." It was just like it was since he was taken into custody Friday afternoon, Lee Oswald doesn't admit to murdering President Kennedy or the officer. However, when he tells them he is a patsy, no one thought about it; if Oswald really was a patsy until after his death. Captain Fritz had enough with Oswald and was ready to get on with his transfer. An officer told Lee it was chilly outside and had offered him a white coat or a black sweater. Oswald chose the sweater. They then handcuff Oswald to detective Jim Leavelle who was one of the detectives who escorted Oswald out. Jim Leavelle is a former Dallas homicide detective who was escorting Lee Harvey Oswald through Dallas Police Headquarters when Oswald was shot by Jack Ruby. Leavelle recalls joking to Oswald before the transfer he said, "Lee if anybody shoots at you I hope they're as good as a shot as you are", meaning they shoot Oswald and not him. Oswald kind of smiled and said, "I think you are being melodramatic nobody is going to shoot at me." Leavelle was shocked about 3 minutes later, he didn't think somebody was going to actually shoot Oswald. He was trying to talk to Oswald while they waited for the ambulance to get there but he was unconscious and probably not going to survive. Jim Leavelle knew Jack Ruby for a number of years and noticed him as he emerged from the crowd of people. Jack Ruby is taken into police custody and Oswald lays in the ground while they waited for the ambulance, slowly slipping away from his gunshot wound in his lower abdomen. The ambulance arrived and Oswald was quickly put in the back of the ambulance with detective Leavelle. Oswald was rushed to Parkland Memorial Hospital. When they arrived at Parkland doctors demanded he was not rushed to trauma room one. They put him in trauma room two because they didn't want him to die in the same room as President Kennedy. They ended up opening Oswald's chest and massaged his heart by hand while detectives were yelling in his face "did you do it" but Oswald didn't move or say a word. With President Kennedy and his accused killer dead America is left in the dark. What happened on that shocking day? Friday November 22nd President Kennedy is murdered in the streets of Dallas, Texas as he campaigns for his re-election in 1964. Dallas Police are certain they have the man who was involved in both murders on that dark afternoon in Texas. The suspect does not admit to anything and denies all questions asked but he is also a suspicious young man who has been to the Soviet Union, has attempted an assassination before and who supported Cuba. Our beloved President who fought for his country and then served it for 1,000 days was killed. His accused killer was shot down. We do not know if Oswald was a patsy or who reportedly set Oswald up in the Kennedy assassination, but we do know Oswald had a big passion for politics and political leaders. No one is alive today to speak up. Lee Harvey Oswald "the patsy" claims it wasn't him. He was never tried for the crime and therefore there will forever be questions about that awful November day in Dallas Texas. Was Lee Oswald just a patsy?

Chapter 11

The Journey Back to Washington

Mrs. Kennedy didn't want to do anything but get back to Washington. She wanted to get home and get through the next few days that were going to be heartbreaking. They get to Parkland Hospital Governor Connolly is rushed inside first, while Mrs. Kennedy and Kennedy's aids already knew the outcome of Kennedy's wounds. It took agents and doctors a while to convince Mrs. Kennedy to let them take the president inside when they did they rush Kennedy inside to trauma room one. Mrs. Kennedy held her husband because she knew Jack was dead. They get the president on the table and take his clothes off. There was no breath sounds and no pulse. Doctors however, found he had a heartbeat. A tube is immediately placed in his neck for air and doctors called for someone to find out Kennedy's blood type. They did everything they possibly could. Finally one of the doctors goes in the trauma room and goes to the very end of the table and looked inside the president's head and made the final decision that the president was dead and there was nothing they can do. His brain was gone and there was no saving him. They had nothing to work with on the operating table. At 1:00 Kennedy is dead, even though doctors believed he died before then due to his condition of his wounds. Then, still in shock secret service, doctors, nurses, Dallas Police, and Mrs. Kennedy all watched as they close the casket with their beloved president inside of it. Secret service had already rushed Vice President Lyndon Johnson and Ladybird back to air force one. Both the secret service and Vice President Johnson thought that this was an international communist conspiracy and they weren't sure if there was another gunman out there waiting to take a shot at Lyndon Johnson as well. Vice President Johnson agreed to go back to air force one but he refused to leave Dallas Love Field Airport without Mrs. Kennedy and the casket carrying the President. Secret Service was in a rush to get the president's body and Mrs. Kennedy back to air force one as soon as possible to get them both back home to Washington. After Kennedy's body is put in the casket the agents were ready to get him back to D.C. Agents closed the casket slowly as they watched to see their president one last time. Mrs. Kennedy told secret service she wasn't going anywhere without her husband. She was going where ever they had to take the casket. Lyndon Johnson had told secret service he wasn't going anywhere without Mrs. Kennedy and the body of President Kennedy. Well for one thing Johnson had to get back to Washington. Johnson was now the chief executive and had a job to fill and Mrs. Kennedy had to get back to Washington to not only see her children, but to get away from the horrific tragedy she had just been through. When they got back to the plane the casket was too big to fit through the door so they had to take some of the handles off to get the casket on Air Force One. President Kennedy is placed in the back of the plane. Mrs. Kennedy goes in the back to freshen herself up. A judge from Texas, Judge Sarah T. Hughes was aboard the plane and ready to give Lyndon Johnson the oath of office for the Presidency of the United States. Lyndon Johnson wanted Mrs. Kennedy by his side as he took the oath. Some of President Kennedy's political aids who weren't a fan of Johnson during the Kennedy administration to begin with thought that had to be the worst possible thing to do to Mrs. Kennedy. To have the poor First Lady stand there and listen to the same oath her husband took three years earlier and just been assassinated right next to her earlier that afternoon, as she held his body all the way to the hospital and tried to hold his head together thinking there was maybe something that the doctor could have done for him. It was already a horrible day for Mrs. Kennedy. Mrs. Kennedy however, agreed to be there when Johnson took the oath. Secret Service and Johnson's wife Ladybird offered for her to change her clothes but Mrs. Kennedy still wanted to stay in her bloodstained outfit for the United States and the rest of the world to see what had happened to her husband. At 2:38 p.m. that afternoon just a couple of hours after President Kennedy is killed Lyndon Johnson is sworn in and becomes the 36th President of the United States. After Johnson took the oath he kissed Mrs. Kennedy and then his wife. He then gave out his first order as President to get Air Force One back to Washington. For a while it was silent on the plane everyone was shocked, confused, and simply all wanted to know why it happened. JFK got to Texas ready to make a difference for the state and left Texas in a bronze wooden casket. On the way back to Washington Mrs. Kennedy started talking about her husband's funeral. She wanted it to be the way John Kennedy would want it. She wanted the country to remember him for who he was. During the ride back to

Washington Mrs. Kennedy was asked if she had ever tried scotch and she never had scotch. Staff on the plane offered her a glass and told her they thought it was a good time for her to try it. It was her very first time having it. Mrs. Kennedy was anxious to get back so they can do her husband's autopsy. Johnson had ordered that news men will be allowed at Andrew's Air Force Base when they land in Washington. Mrs. Kennedy and Kennedy's aids didn't like that at all. Air Force One arrives at Andrew's Air Force Base near 7:00 p.m. that evening where cameras and people were there waiting to see the body of their President arrive back home. Bobby Kennedy was there waiting for Mrs. Kennedy and when the plane got in he ran to it and entered the plane through the front to find Mrs. Kennedy. Jackie, Bobby, Kennedy's aids, and the casket came off the air plane where marines were awaiting to put their president in the ambulance. President Kennedy's aids had asked if they can carry the body of their former commander and chief as they serve him one last time. Mrs. Kennedy and Bobby Kennedy also get into the ambulance and citizens watched as the ambulance made its way to Bethesda Naval Hospital for the President's autopsy. Mrs. Kennedy, Bobby, and the Kennedy aids and staff sat in the waiting room at the hospital and watched the news as they waited for medical examiners to finish the autopsy. The autopsy was finished early the next morning and President Kennedy's casket arrived back home at the White House for the last time at 4:30 a.m. November 23rd. He was brought inside where he lay in state for staff members who worked with him and Mrs. Kennedy to pay their respects. While traditionally when a president lies in state an armor guard faces out to protect their commander and chief. Mrs. Kennedy had asked if the armor guards can face the casket so the president didn't look like he was alone. They had done what the former first lady had said and they faced their President instead. President Lyndon Johnson order a day of prayer for the former President. The flag at the white house was flown at half-staff. President Kennedy had once quoted "A man may die, nations may rise and fall, but an idea lives on." The nation had lost their President who loved his country, who fought for his country, and who passed the torch to a new generation as said in his inaugural address. The funeral of the late President John F. Kennedy was held on Monday November 25, 1963 Kennedy's casket was place on the same catapult that President Abraham Lincoln's body was carried on almost 100 years ago. Hundreds of people lined the streets of Washington in silence. Not one word was heard as citizens say their final good-bye to their beloved President John Fitzgerald Kennedy. Pennsylvania Avenue was packed with hundreds of people as it was just three years earlier. President Kennedy the 4th child of Joe and Rose Kennedy to die tragically has left a symbol of dignity, and courage. A man who once said "we will land a man on the moon." A man who once said "Change is the law of life and those who look only to the past and present are certain to miss the future." A man who once said "Ask not what your country can do for you, ask what you can do for your country." He was a man of many words and those words live on in all Americans. President Kennedy's casket makes its way from the White House to the Capitol and from the Capitol to Arlington National Cemetery, it makes way passed his family and his young son John Jr. salutes his father and president. At Arlington, Mrs. Kennedy and Bobby Kennedy light the internal flame for the 35th President. It was the start of a difficult journey for Mrs. Kennedy and the rest of the Kennedy family.

Chapter 12

Jackie Kennedy

Jacqueline Kennedy Onassis was one of the most admired first ladies ever, she was beautiful. Like John Kennedy, she came from a wealthy family her father died and Jackie didn't really have the best relationship with her mother. On September 12, 1953 Jackie married Senator John F. Kennedy. People called it the wedding of the century, Jackie wanted a small wedding but it was a public and political event. 900 people attended church and 1,200 people were at their reception. Both republicans and democrats came to celebrate the new young couple. Their marriage became a rocky one due to Jack's off reported womanizing. Jackie sat down with her father-in-law Joe Kennedy in Hyannis Port and told him she was going to file for divorce. Joe had talked Jackie out of it and paid her one million dollars to stay with Jack. Joe said to her when he runs for president in 1960 he was going to need her to help him win. Jackie stayed by the senator's side despite him having secret affairs behind her back. In 1954 Senator Kennedy had spinal surgery and had slipped into a coma a priest came to give him last rights but he came out of the coma and was back in the senate months later with crutches. After a while he was back on his feet and looking better. A year later in 1955 Jackie had suffered a miscarriage and was recovering. In 1956 she gave birth to a stillborn a baby girl they had named Arabella. They had gone through a lot of tragic and Mrs. Kennedy relaxed as she recovered from the loss of her daughter. Their lives turned around in November of 1957 when Mrs. Kennedy gave birth to their first daughter Caroline. It was wonderful for her and the senator. They went on to raise Caroline as the senator worked many hours. He confide to Jackie that he wanted to become president and kicked off his campaign for the 1960 election. Mrs. Kennedy and the whole Kennedy family were by his side every day to help him. On election night Kennedy beat Vice President Nixon and was now president-elect. The next day during his victory speech he told all Americans he needed their help to move the country safely through the 1960's he then said that his wife and him prepare for a new administration and a new baby. Mrs. Kennedy was pregnant with their second child. The couple didn't know what they were having. Mrs. Kennedy said she would name the boy after her husbands but they didn't have any ideas for a girl's name yet. On November 25, 1960 Mrs. Kennedy went into labor and had given birth to a son John F. Kennedy Jr. Caroline and John Jr. were the only two surviving children of John and Jackie Kennedy. After Jackie had the baby they flew down to Palm Beach Florida where Kennedy thought of people to start picking for his administration. On January 20, 1961 Mrs. Kennedy watched as her husband was sworn in as the 35th President of the United States. They had brought style and class to the White House the country loved everything about the first family. The family became known as Camelot. The White House years were both good and bad for the couple. JFK faced a lot of problems during his presidency, politically and personally. Mrs. Kennedy stood by her husband at his worst but left at various occasions with the kids to go to Virginia during John's womanizing behind her back. She made it clear to him she had many private humiliations but she did not want to have them in front of the American people. President Kennedy had slowed down with his off reported womanizing due to FBI director J. Edgar Hoover stopping him. He loved Jackie and realized it wasn't only him who made a difference in this country but her as well. In 1963 Mrs. Kennedy was pregnant with their third child. It was a beautiful blessing for her and President Kennedy. JFK worked hard the year of 1963 not only to be a better husband but to do right for his country that he loved and wanted to run again come 1964. The Kennedy White House was going well and the President had high hopes for the nation. Early August the President got an unexpected call from Hyannis Port that Mrs. Kennedy had gone into labor early. President Kennedy, his aids, and Bobby Kennedy left for Hyannis Port. Doctors came out and told Jack that his son Patrick had a respiratory problem. Jack went in to see Patrick and did nothing other than pray for him to get better quick. Mrs. Kennedy knew what was going on but didn't know how bad it really was. 2 days later little Patrick died at just 2 days old. After Patrick's death John's "women problem" came to an end. Mrs. Kennedy and the President left the hospital following the death of their newborn son and headed to Washington where Mrs. Kennedy got packed and ready for a trip she was taking for herself to Greece to recover from losing her son. President Kennedy along with his two children Caroline and John Jr. spent the rest of their summer in Hyannis Port at the Kennedy compound.

When Mrs. Kennedy arrived back home from her vacation she was greeted by her husband and children. The motorcade took the family back to the White House. On the way back John tells Jackie he is ready to campaign for the 1964 election he wanted to go campaign in Texas because he was afraid of losing them in the election. Mrs. Kennedy told him she would campaign where ever he wanted to go. Mrs. Kennedy was still upset about losing Patrick but she and Jack became closer together and he wanted to be the man she deserved to have. It was the closest they ever been in a long time. In November of 1963 JFK went to Texas for two days to deliver 5 speeches in 5 cities and towns in Texas. Mrs. Kennedy came along which made the crowd cheer louder. The public hadn't seen Mrs. Kennedy since the death of her son Patrick. They stayed at a hotel in Fort Worth the night of November 21st. The next morning Mrs. Kennedy laid out her beautiful pink suit for their ride through Dallas that day. President Kennedy went outside to deliver a speech to the people outside the hotel and then back inside to deliver a speech to the people inside the hotel where dozens of people were their waiting for him to give a speech at a breakfast. When he arrived outside to greet the crowd and make his speech the crowd cheered for Jackie asking where she was and President Kennedy said that "Mrs. Kennedy is upstairs organizing herself. She takes longer but she looks better than we do." The president finished his speech and headed inside for the breakfast where Vice President Johnson and his wife Ladybird were there and Governor Connolly and Mrs. Connolly was there as well. President Kennedy stood by the podium as the crowd at the breakfast applaud their president. Mrs. Kennedy wasn't sure if she was going to attend the breakfast or not. The president wanted her there and asked her secret service agent Clint Hill to send the message to Mrs. Kennedy that the president wanted her to come downstairs for the breakfast. Mrs. Kennedy did agree to join her husband at the breakfast in the lobby. She came down with Mr. Hill and took a seat next to the president. The president began his speech and said to the audience, "2 years ago I introduced myself in Paris by saying I was the man who accompanied Mrs. Kennedy to Paris, and I am getting that same sensation as I travel around Texas." The crowd laughed at his joke and the President continued what would be the last speech he would ever give. President and Mrs. Kennedy left the breakfast to then get in the motorcade where it will take them back to Air Force One for the flight to Dallas. They arrive in Dallas and the door to Air Force One opened. Mrs. Kennedy stepped out first and then the President of the United States the crowd went absolutely wild. They were ecstatic. Mrs. Kennedy was handed a beautiful bouquet of roses. The president immediately went up to the fence where the crowd was and began shaking hands with the people by the fence at Dallas Love Field. Mrs. Kennedy went along with her husband and shook hands with the crowd also. It was a huge and friendly crowd. After they both made their way down the fence they walked over to the presidential motorcade where Governor and Mrs. Connolly were already there awaiting them. Mrs. Kennedy stepped into the car first and then her husband and the motorcade started to make its way through downtown Dallas on that bright and sunny day. The motorcade made its way slowly through the streets of Dallas so all citizens could see the first couple. The president waved proudly as well as Mrs. Kennedy who was very happy she decided to travel with her husband on the campaign trial. The crowd was big on Main Street there were people all over the street and hanging out of windows all cheering for their president and first lady. The motorcade turned onto

Houston Street just before they made the turn onto Elm Street where Mrs. Kennedy's life would change forever she leaned next to the president and told him she loved him. Moments later the president laid helplessly in his wife's lap bleeding from his head, Mrs. Kennedy was in shock as her husband was killed. As Mrs. Kennedy got back into the motorcade with her secret service agent right behind her Clint Hill who ran to the motorcade the president's body fell into her lap with his face up and his eye were fixed she covered his head and face and tried to hold his head together as they raced to Parkland Hospital. Mrs. Kennedy ran inside the hospital by her husband's side until they got to the trauma room and they told her she couldn't go any further. They got her a chair to sit on outside the trauma room where they were working on the president. Mrs. Kennedy waited outside the trauma room with blood dripping down her leg, her pink suit was completely covered with blood and her white gloves she wore had blood all over them. Nurses asked her to change but she refused she wanted everyone to see what happened to her husband. Doctors got him in a casket and then in an ambulance and Mrs. Kennedy got in next to her husband's body still in shock and still covered from head to toe in blood from her husband's murder that afternoon. The ambulance arrived back at Love Field where secret service brought the casket containing their former president onto Air Force One. Mrs. Kennedy walked onto the plane after the casket and went in the back where she was crying and trying to freshen herself up for Vice President Lyndon Johnson to take the oath of office for the presidency. The ride back was pretty silent everyone still in shock of what took place on what was supposed to be an ordinary day for the president, Mrs. Kennedy, and his staff. Mrs. Kennedy sat next to her husband's casket the way home. It was a long night for Mrs. Kennedy, after they got through with the president's autopsy and got his casket ready to be placed at the White House they got the President's casket in the ambulance where he would go home for the last time. It was 4:30 Friday morning when his body arrived. A military honor guard stood by the casket as the president's body laid there with the American flag draped over the casket. The next day Sunday November 24, 1963 the casket carrying the 35th President was brought to the capitol building where he would lie in state as American's came to pay their respects. Pennsylvania Avenue was packed up and down the street with hundreds and thousands of citizens who were lined up and down that same street three years earlier. At the capitol Mrs. Kennedy and Caroline went over to the casket and knelt down beside it. Mrs. Kennedy kissed her husband's casket and Caroline touched it. They both then walked back to their seats. The following day President Kennedy's casket made its way to his final resting place at Arlington National Cemetery. The casket walked by the Kennedy brothers, Mrs. Kennedy and their children as his casket was brought by his son John Jr. who he had called John-John stepped out and proudly saluted his father he would never know. After President Kennedy was laid to rest that afternoon Mrs. Kennedy went back to the white house where she had a birthday party planned for John Jr. who turned three years old that day of his late father's funeral. She made the event as normal as possible for the children and it went very well. John Jr. had a nice party even though it was one of the saddest days in America and he was too young to realize how sad it was and what an impact his father made on every person the past three years. President Johnson and Mrs. Johnson let Mrs. Kennedy and the children stay in the white house another two weeks and let them take their time to get their things together before moving out. After packing up and leaving the house they stayed and were known to live at Mrs. Kennedy's home in New York. Mrs. Kennedy still did her best at keeping her children out of the public eye and keeping them safe. To her, she felt as though if people were killing Kennedy's her children could be targets as well. It was what would be a long recovery for the former first lady after watching her husband being murdered right next to her. How did Mrs. Kennedy manage to sit next to her husband watching him slowly die in those final moments with his head profusely bleeding and brain all over him, his wife, and the rest of the motorcade? I think people all over America couldn't imagine Mrs. Kennedy's heartbreak and disbelief, the events that took place in Dallas was something so shocking. Mrs. Kennedy like anyone else lost her husband, but that day in November she lost him through tragedy that will forever be a day the Kennedy family young and old won't forget and it will forever be one of America's most shocking days in history. Mrs. Kennedy was very brave that day.

Chapter 13

Tragedy and Onassis

Tragedy ended one Kennedy's presidency and would later stop another Kennedy from becoming president. They were a charming young family who helped our country. They did no wrong in their political careers. Why were the Kennedy's targets and victims of assassinations? From investigating organized crime to assassinations, and car and plane accidents the family lived in fear constantly wondering why tragedy kept happening to the family. Tragedy struck them horrifically and made them realize life is short and you need to live it with family. They stayed close as a family after the 1960's despite the tragedy of the Kennedy brothers John and Bobby. John Kennedy was a man of many words, a man who served in the war and gathered all his crew members and keeping them safe, a young man who ran for the presidency of the United States and held the title for only 1,000 days. In those 1,000 days Kennedy accomplished a lot with his father's political background and the help of his younger brother Bobby Kennedy who he made attorney general got him through every day of his presidency. Bobby stuck by John through everything he never left his side and was there through every political problem he was facing. The brothers were very close and Kennedy knew he needed Bobby by him throughout his presidency and in 1964 for his re-election. Bobby Kennedy was a hard worker and kept up on the political problems they were facing. Bobby got along with everyone in Kennedy's administration except his brothers Vice President Lyndon Johnson. Johnson was tough but so was Bobby but no matter what the situation was or what was going on they always seem to disagree with one another. Johnson didn't like Bobby and Bobby despised Johnson but they both kept the peace for the same reason. The president. On November 22, 1963 when the news got back to the White House that President Kennedy had been shot Mrs. Kennedy's secret service agent was talking to his boss when an operator cut in and said that the attorney general wanted to talk to Hill. Bobby asked how bad it really was and after Hill said it was as bad as it can get Bobby hung up the phone. When Lyndon Johnson got back to Air Force One he called Bobby Kennedy to see how the oath of office had to be done and if he could find someone to do it on the plane before they got back to

Washington. Johnson told Kennedy he thought the country shouldn't go without a president in case they were facing an international communist conspiracy. Although Bobby thought Johnson was simply trying to overpower him. Bobby knew all that was on Johnson's mind was simply becoming president. Bobby knew then he didn't see his political career as attorney general going any farther without his brother as president. Bobby got in touch with Judge Sara T. Hughes and she swore Johnson in as the 36th President of the United States on Air Force One before the plane left for Washington. Nine months into the Johnson administration Robert Kennedy resigned as attorney general. He ran for a seat in the U.S. Senate representing New York. Kennedy drew attention in Congress early on as the brother of President Kennedy, which set him apart from other senators. He drew more than fifty senators as spectators when he delivered a speech in the Senate on nuclear proliferation in June 1965. Bobby saw his brother as a guide to help him in the senate. Kennedy was very busy in the senate and also with the family. Not only was he the father of his eight children he had he was also now the father and guide for Caroline and John Jr. as well. After his brother was assassinated Mrs. Kennedy leaned on

Bobby for a lot and called him late at night or during the day when she was upset and he left his own wife and children to be with her. He was everything to Jackie. He was as close as she would get to Jack and was there for her through the worst every day. Jackie just simply couldn't imagine life without him. It was reported that Jackie and Bobby had an affair and though no one actually knows if it is true or not but seeing they were Kennedy's it probably was a true statement seeing they spent so much time together and Jackie always wanted to be with Bobby. Bobby had pretty much not only played the role of father for the kids but also the role of husband for Jackie as well. In 1968 Kennedy decided to run for president to carry on for his beloved brother John. It was a big event for him and the family to be campaigning once again for another president in the family. Although Joe made all the decisions during Jack's campaign and was the one who called all the shots he was in a wheelchair after suffering from his stroke when Jack was president, Bobby knew what a great campaigner his mother was and the stories she could tell so he took her on the campaign trail and she helped him for the upcoming election hoping her son would get into office and carry on what her older son started in 1961. Bobby and the Kennedy family had high hopes for what was coming and the country was more than excited to see yet another Kennedy son running for office. Camelot was back and ready to keep the Kennedy legacy going. The Senator from New York was doing great. The Kennedy family worked hard day and night as they did eight years earlier to get Bobby every single vote both Democrat and Republican. In 1960 when Jack won the election Bobby who was then Jack's campaign manager sat down with his father Joe and told him after this he wanted to be Governor of Massachusetts and spend more time with his wife Ethel and his children. Joe agreed as they sat in his office on election night. Joe thanked Bobby for making his dream come true making Jack President of the United States. The following day when the family was all together Joe had thought about what Bobby had said to him about becoming Governor of Massachusetts and thought his son deserved better after getting his brother elected as president. Joe made a list of people for Jack to think about for his cabinet and Joe had Bobby down as attorney general. When Bobby saw his name on the paper he confronted his father and told him he didn't want the job. Joe wanted Bobby in the White House to help out

Jack. Joe knew Jack was going to need someone he can talk to and lean on and that was Bobby. He wanted Bobby to keep an eye on Jack. Joe also said it would be great for Bobby to do so he could follow Jack in 1968. Bobby wanted no part of it and repeatedly told Joe and Jack he wanted to stay in Massachusetts. Ethel thought it would be a great job for him as well as his mother Rose. Rose had said to Bobby "there is no man at your age who wouldn't accept this job" Jack jokingly said to her "yes there is Robert Kennedy." Bobby talked privately with his father about the situation as well as Jack. He was determined to stay in Massachusetts with his family. After talking to his father, his brother, and his wife Bobby agreed to take the job and stick by his brother's side as he did throughout his campaign. And so Jack appointed Bobby as his attorney general. Although Bobby had no experience in any state or federal court, causing the president to joke, "I can't see that it's wrong to give him a little legal experience before he goes out to practice law." However the New York Times and other magazine companies had written on their front page calling Bobby inexperienced and unqualified for the job. However, Kennedy was hardly a novice as a lawyer, and he gained significant experience conducting investigations and questioning witnesses as a Justice Department attorney and Senate committee counsel and staff director. Bobby enjoyed his job and kept it until his brother's assassination. 1968 he enters the race for president. America thought that the country would be the way it was eight years earlier when his older brother John entered the race for president. Bobby was as confident as any Kennedy running for public office and so was the country. Although Joe Kennedy was confide to a wheelchair he kept up with his son's campaign on television and supported him in the background. Bobby's campaign was going great until June of 1968. Kennedy scored major victory when he won the California primary. It was after midnight June 5, 1968 Bobby and his with Ethel who was pregnant with their 11th child Rory Kennedy were in Los Angeles on the campaign trail and things were going nothing but great for Bobby. After his speech he and Ethel left the ball room and went through the kitchen being told it was a shortcut to the press room. In the crowded kitchen Kennedy turned to his left to shake hands with one of the busboys when Sirhan Sirhan opened fired with a 22 caliber revolver. Kennedy was hit three times and five other people were seriously wounded. As Bobby laid there mortally wounded people cradled his head and placed a rosary in his hand. He turned to his wife and asked, "Is everyone else ok?" They all tried to keep him with them as best they could until help arrived. When paramedics arrived and lifted Kennedy up on the stretcher Kennedy whispered, "Don't lift me." And those were the last words Bobby Kennedy would ever speak. He lost consciousness shortly after that. He was rushed to Los Angeles Receiving Hospital where he underwent neurosurgery to remove the bullet and bone fragments from his brain. He then slipped into a coma where the family had to make the tough decision of letting him go. After the family said their final good-bye's Robert F. Kennedy was pronounced dead at 1:44 a.m. on June 6, 1968 nearly 26 hours after the shooting. Bobby's death, like President Kennedy's assassination back in 1963 have both to this day been the subject of conspiracy theories. Kennedy's body was brought back to Manhattan where he laid in state at St. Patrick's Cathedral. A mass was held at 10:00 a.m. on June 8th. The service was attended by the Kennedy family, President Johnson and his wife Ladybird and members of Johnson's administration. A eulogy was read by Ted Kennedy the only surviving son of Joe and

Rose. After the mass Kennedy's body was transported by a special private train to Washington D.C. the train finally arrived there at 9:10 p.m. June 8th. Robert Kennedy was buried along with his brother President Kennedy at Arlington National Cemetery. On June 9th President Lyndon Johnson declared an official national day of mourning. Jackie Kennedy couldn't believe that this was happening again. Bobby was her go-to person and his life tragically ended the same way as Jack's bringing back memories to her of that awful day in Dallas. After Bobby's funeral Ted, Joe and Rose's youngest son and only living son talked about running for president he was going to enter when Rose and the rest of the Kennedy family put an end to it. Rose told Ted he had one job and that was not only being the father of his own children, but Jack and Bobby's as well and that was the only obligation that matters. Ted agreed with everyone not to run. After what the family had went through and not one Kennedy brother killed in office but two scared the Kennedys. For Jackie it was different she thought that if they were killing Kennedy's her children could be targets. It scared her and she wanted to get out of the country. For a while she had been talking to Aristotle Onassis a rich Greek shipping man who made more money than anyone. He made the Kennedy's look bad with all the money he had. Mrs. Kennedy had been talking to him and told him how upset and scared she was that both Jack and Bobby were both gone. Onassis came to see Jackie and it wasn't long before people realized they were together. Mrs. Kennedy was very over protective of her children and wanted them to be safe. Onassis told her to come back to Greece with him, he told her he would protect them all and keep them safe there. Mrs. Kennedy wanted him however to go to Hyannis Port and meet the Kennedy's. He told her he knew they hated him but for her he would go. The family always got together for picnics at Hyannis Port and Mrs. Kennedy told Rose she was bringing Aristotle or "Ari" as Jackie called him to the get together to meet everyone. As Onassis sat with Rose he talked to her about marrying Jackie. Rose and the rest of the family were catholic. She knew Onassis had been divorced and Rose told him that was not accepted in the church. He told Rose that he knew there will always be a place in Jackie's heart for her son. Rose saw how happy Jackie was with Onassis and her and her son Ted both agreed she hadn't been that happy since she lost Jack. Rose knew if that's what would make her happy then she and the rest of the family will have to accept it. Jackie saw enough tragedy in the family and she feared there would be more. She only wanted the best for her children, she wanted them to live normal lives like other children. On October 20, 1968 almost five months after Bobby's assassination Jackie married her long-time friend Aristotle Onassis. They got married in Scorpios, Onassis's Private Island in Greece. He provided safety for her and her children away from the United States where Jackie feared they can be the next targets of an assassination. Ari had two children a son Alexander and a daughter Christina. There was a lot of tension between his kids and Jackie. His children had hoped he would remarry their mother after leaving his relationship with Maria Callas. His son Alexander once said, "My father loves names and Jackie loves money." Although they were in Greece Mrs. Kennedy did want her children to still have a relationship with the Kennedy's they were their family. They often went back to see them and Jackie stayed close to Ted. She developed a close relationship with him and from then on he was involved in a lot of her public appearances. Jackie and Ari's relationship started to become a rocky one. Onassis's son Alexander then died in a plane crash in 1973 after that

Ari's health started to go downhill. He and Jackie were in the middle of a divorce and it was almost finalized when Onassis died of respiratory failure at the age of 69 in Paris March 15, 1975. Their divorce was never final and Jackie was left to the Onassis estate but his daughter Christina wasn't having it. She didn't want her father's estate to go to Jackie and her children. After two years of legal wrangling Jackie Kennedy accepted a settlement of $26 million from Christina Onassis and waived all other claims to the Onassis estate. After the death of her second husband, Jackie Kennedy Onassis returned to the United States permanently splitting her time between Manhattan, Hyannis Port at the Kennedy Compound, and Martha's Vineyard. She kept a close eye on her children and made sure they were safe at all times. Her children got older and went on to do their own things and have their own careers. They made Jackie proud and the family knew they also made their father proud as well. Even though John Jr. was only three when his father died and is known by all for saluting his father's casket as a young boy made him popular since that sad day in Washington. Caroline who was older and had more memories with her father adored him as a child and carried on his legacy when she was older. In December 1993 Jackie Kennedy was diagnosed with Hodgkin Lymphoma. She began chemotherapy in January 1994. By March the cancer had spread to her spinal cord, brain, and by May it had spread to her liver. Mrs. Kennedy died in her Manhattan apartment at the age of 64 at 10:15 p.m. in her sleep. On May 19, 1994. John F. Kennedy Jr. announced his mother's death to the press the next morning. On May 23, 1994 a funeral mass was held for her a few blocks away from her apartment at the Church of Saint Ignatius Loyola, the Catholic Parish where she was baptized in 1929. She was brought to her final resting place at Arlington National Cemetery where she was buried next to her husband, President John F. Kennedy, her son Patrick, and her stillborn daughter Arabella. A eulogy was given at her graveside by President Clinton. Mrs. Kennedy was a charming and one of the most admired first ladies. She passed away leaving a legacy behind.

Chapter 14

The Prince of Camelot's Tragic Death

John Fitzgerald Kennedy Jr. was the prince of Camelot,
born November 25, 1960. He was the son of a President
and an admirable First Lady, but he became known simply
as John-John as his father called him. He spent his early
years living in the White House and in the public eye. John
was little and spent a lot of time with his parents. He was
the first son born to a President-elect. He was known for
that historic picture of him playing under the desk in the
oval office as his father worked. Mrs. Kennedy tried to
keep her children from being in the public eye but Jack
saw it was good especially for the Kennedy White House
for the country to see the first family. The country adored
JFK Jr. In November of 1963 President Kennedy was
starting to campaign for the 1964 presidential election. He
and Jackie were traveling to Texas to help get him votes.
As they were ready to board Marine One to go to Andrews
Air force Base little John Jr. was upset. He didn't want his
parents to leave him. As he sat there and cried as his
parents had to leave his father kissed him good-bye and

said "it's okay we will be back in time for your birthday party." President Kennedy and Mrs. Kennedy boarded Marine One. Sadly that was the last time John Jr. would see his father alive. John turned three years old November 25, 1963 the same day of his father's funeral. The little boy reportedly walked around the White House upset because he didn't have anyone to play with. The President's funeral was sad for all, it was the day John-John captured the nation's heart when he touchingly saluted his father's casket. That iconic image left the country in tears. John, his sister Caroline, and Jackie left the White House two weeks following the assassination. President Johnson gave them time to pack and get ready to move out. John-John was close to the Kennedy family and became even closer after his father died. He did a lot especially with his uncle Bobby Kennedy. Bobby became a father figure to John and Caroline after Jack died. After Bobby's assassination in 1968 John-John moved to Greece with his sister when their mother married Aristotle Onassis. John was eight years old when Bobby died and he was old enough to know what had happen and he was heartbroken to lose his uncle who was there for him his entire childhood. He did travel back to the United States so he could see his family and his Kennedy cousins. Ted Kennedy the only surviving son of Joe and Rose became a father figure not only to John-John and Caroline but for all of Bobby's children as well. John-John came back to the United States following the death of Onassis in 1975. He lived with his mother and sister in New York where he attended high school and college. John's mother died in May 1994. He reported her death to the press the next morning. She was buried with his father at Arlington National Cemetery. Kennedy Jr. married Carolyn Bessette on September 21, 1996, the couple honeymooned in Turkey. When they got home from their honeymoon a mass of reporters was waiting on their doorstep. Being married to John Kennedy Jr. was a big adjustment seeing Carolyn was a private citizen before she married him. Carolyn was badly disappointed by the constant attention from the paparazzi. Every day the reporters followed them where ever they went. John started to take flying lessons at Flight Safety Academy in Vero Beach, Florida. In April 1998, he received his pilot's license, which he had aspired to since he was a child. Jackie Kennedy held him back from getting his pilot's license, she was scared of what could happen to him. It scared her because his uncle Joe died in a plane crash in 1944. The eldest son of Joe and Rose. John Jr. went for lessons after his mother passed away. John sat in many planes as a child especially when his father was president. He loved everything about them and dreamed to one day fly a plane. He got his license to fly and couldn't be more excited. He flew a small plane that he purchased on April 28, 1999 from Air Bound Aviation. On July 16, 1999 Kennedy was departing from Fairfield, New Jersey to attend the wedding of his cousin Rory Kennedy, the youngest daughter to Bobby and Ethel in Hyannis Port, Massachusetts. Kennedy Jr. typically didn't fly at night considering he never did and wasn't licensed to. He wanted to take off early enough before it got dark, he left just before dark with his wife Carolyn and her sister Lauren. Carolyn and Lauren were passengers in the second row seats. It started to get dark making it difficult for Kennedy to fly. John Jr. checked in with the control tower at Martha's Vineyard Airport. The plane was considered missing as it failed to arrive on schedule. The following day the Kennedy family was very worried about John not arriving. As news got out that John, his wife, and sister-in-law were missing officials and the Kennedy family weren't hopeful about finding them alive. A black suitcase belonging to Bessette was recovered from the Atlantic Ocean. President Bill Clinton gave his support and prayers to the Kennedy family during the search for the prince of Camelot, and his passengers. On July 18th everyone lost hope for finding them. July 19th fragments of Kennedy's plane were found. The search continued day after day all day long. It was so sad for the Kennedy's and the country. Everyone knew the outcome of all of this wasn't going to be good. On July 21st the three bodies were recovered and brought by motorcade to the county medical examiner's office. Divers found Carolyn and Lauren's bodies near the twisted and broken fuselage while Kennedy's body was still strapped into the pilot's seat. After hearing about his plane missing all over the news people all over the country feared it was going to end like this. July 23, 1999 a memorial service was held for Kennedy at the Church of St. Thomas More, it was the parish Kennedy often attended with his mother and sister. Thousands of mourners attended including President Bill Clinton. President Clinton presented the family with a photo album of John and Carolyn visiting the white house from the previous year. Sadly another Kennedy died tragically. John's uncle Ted Kennedy began thinking about this so called "The Kennedy Curse" everyone talks about. He started to believe that when his incident happened in Chappaquiddick. After John Jr.'s death Ted had other thoughts about it. However it has been argued that the events were normal for a large extended family like that can experience that kind of tragedy. Many people still talk about and think about "The Kennedy Curse." It was a sad year for America to lose the Prince of Camelot who many Americans hoped and believe John Jr. would walk into his father's footsteps and run for President of the United States. We are left unknown if John-John would enter politics as a young Kennedy.

Chapter 15

A Look Back On That November Weekend

Arlington National Cemetery and the final resting place of one of America's greatest heroes. Each year three and a half million people come to the cemetery to pay respects for this man. They also come to ponder one of the greatest murder mysteries of all time. November 22, 1963 Americas nightmare on Elm Street was about to begin. John F. Kennedy was assassinated in Dallas, Texas. On the corner of Elm and Houston street a gunman Lee Harvey Oswald was about to start shooting from the 6th floor of the Texas School Book Depository. Oswald was eventually caught and question by Dallas police unfortunately they couldn't get Oswald to confess. Police had plan to move Oswald from city jail to county jail where they felt it would be easier to protect their prisoner. Shockingly America never had time to consider what really happened on that day in Dallas when another gunshot made a terrible situation even worse. Lee Harvey Oswald the alleged assassin that Dallas Police were sure had killed their president was gunned down by Dallas nightclub owner

Jack Ruby in full view of millions of Americans watching television. There wasn't any evidence given other than that Oswald acted alone. At least that was what the Warren Commission told us. The shooting of the alleged suspect made most Americans realize that there couldn't have been any other reason but that there was some kind of conspiracy behind the Kennedy Assassination. 1964 came in with a sign of relief. Relief that the year had ended in which President Kennedy was killed and that there can be new beginnings. For Jack Ruby there was no way to forget, he spent 1964 in jail his visitors were his family and his lawyers. He tried to commit suicide twice, once he banged his head against a steel wall and stuck his finger into a light socket. There can never be a trial of Lee Harvey Oswald to prove beyond that legal shadow of a doubt if he was the assassin of President Kennedy, a second assassin's bullet took care of that, but it was considered highly important in Washington to use all the evidence that they know to help lift that shadow. The big question was, what kind of man shot Lee Oswald? And why? Something conspiratorial and sinister took place in Dallas more to the case than simply a communist inclined fanatic shooting the president. It was told to believe it really happened the way it was reported to have happen and that belief can be largely founded on the killing of Oswald. Maybe Ruby had a mental breakout when he fired the shot like his lawyers said or maybe he had some motive of a kind. Ruby simply stated that he couldn't help it. It's a bazar story of some strange interplay of faith which somehow interlocked the destinies of John Fitzgerald Kennedy, Lee Oswald, and Jack Ruby. What can be said is Jack Ruby did not help out in anyway in solving Kennedy's assassination. Ruby later said he was distraught over the president's death and that his motive for killing Oswald was from saving Mrs. Kennedy to come back for trial. Some people hypothesized that Ruby was part of a conspiracy. G. Robert Blakey, chief counsel for the House Select Committee on assassinations from 1977 to 1979 said, "The most plausible explanation for the murder of Oswald by Jack Ruby was that Ruby had stalked Oswald on behalf of organized crime." The organized crime Bobby Kennedy was involved in when he was going after all the mobsters. Who is Lee Harvey Oswald? We don't know the whole story we may never know the whole story but we do know his big passion in life was politics. Governor Connolly and Mrs. Connolly were riding in the motorcade with President and Mrs. Kennedy they sat in the jump seats in front of them. When the Car turned the corner from Houston Street onto Elm Street Mrs. Connolly turned to the President and said to him "You can't say Dallas doesn't love you Mr. President." Seconds later the President of the United States was dead. John Kennedy died from the wounds received in an assassination at 12:30 p.m. Governor Connolly who was also wounded in the shooting survived and later on wanted to investigate the president's murder himself. After Governor Connolly ran all his papers for his investigation 10 years after the assassination he and his wife Nellie both agreed Oswald killed the President but it was the result of a conspiracy. Oswald was discharged from the Marines and his discharge papers were signed by Governor Connolly appointed by President Kennedy. Governor Connolly felt he was the target or both men were the targets. Governor John Connolly believes that one gun alone triggered the tragedy with 3 faithful shots. Was Oswald's main target Governor Connolly or both of them? November 25, 1963 three funerals were held that day. President Kennedy's, Officer Tippit's, and Lee Oswald's. Thousands of people lined the streets of Washington and the Capitol building for President Kennedy's, hundreds of people attended officer Tippit's funeral in Dallas. Lee Harvey Oswald's funeral was just his wife, mother, brother, and his two daughters. The six pallbearers who carried his casket were news men. There were not enough relatives or friends to serve as pallbearers. Marguerite Oswald always believed that her son was innocent. She always thought that and she never changed her mind. She always believed that Oswald was a secret agent for the government and told reporters that her son did more for his country than any other living human being. Mrs. Oswald died at the age of 81. Robert Oswald was very shocked to hear on the radio that his brother killed the president of the United States. Police suggested to Robert that he should change his last name and move far away from Dallas as possible. But Robert never did move or change his last name he stayed in Dallas and continued to raise his family there. Robert paid $710.00 for his brother's funeral. Looking back on that dark tragic day in November makes you realize what a standstill the country came to. People all over the country and the world paused to try to put together that the President of the United States had been shot. You see the president and first lady walk down the steps of Air Force One as they arrived in Dallas. Now when you look back at those pictures you feel like whispering, "Watch out, don't get in the motorcade. You don't know what's waiting for you." Kennedy's trip to Dallas was a two day tour and he was supposed to be giving five speeches in five different cities of Texas. The plan on the day of Friday November 22nd was to arrive in Dallas and take the motorcade through downtown Dallas to the Dallas trade mart where Kennedy was going to go there to give a speech at a luncheon and then go to Vice President, Lyndon Johnson's ranch for the night before heading home to Washington in time for John Jr.'s 3rd birthday. Before Kennedy hits the triple underpass to the Dallas Trade Mart Lee Harvey Oswald had other plans for Kennedy that afternoon. The president never made it to the Dallas Trade Mart for the lunch. People there got the news he had been shot and were shocked. The worst thing that can happen in our Democracy is taking place. Jackie Kennedy knew her husband was gone. At that moment the Kennedy presidency ends and Lyndon Johnson who was just two cars behind was technically the President of the United States and he didn't even know it. However Johnson was not aware that this was a rifleman he thought it was fire crackers or a motorcycle backfiring he really wasn't aware that Kennedy had just been shot multiply times in his motorcade. At Parkland Hospital when secret service rush Johnson inside to a secure location they take him right by Kennedy's motorcade where he and Mrs. Kennedy were and Johnson wasn't even able to see what was wrong with Kennedy. Once Johnson got details on Kennedy's condition and what had happened he remained in an unknown location in the hospital while doctors worked on the president. Moments later one of Kennedy's political aids came in the room where Johnson and his wife Ladybird was and said, "Mr. President, we're ready to go to Air Force One." Johnson knew Kennedy was dead. For less than an hour the country was without a functioning commander and chief until Johnson took the oath aboard the plane before leaving for Washington. Kennedy was the youngest president ever elected and was the youngest president to die in office as well. If it could be done to John Kennedy in 1963 it can be done to another president in the future and we can't let that happen. It's not fair for someone to kill the president and then get away with it for more than half a century. The southeast corner window of the Texas School Book Depository is the spot where Lee Harvey Oswald fired the shots into Dealey Plaza striking the president from behind according to the Warren Commission's report. Until now the world is told to accept the Warren Commissions verdict of the murder of John Kennedy. All of the Warren Commission's records were submitted to the National Archives in 1964. The unpublished portion of those records was initially sealed for 75 years (to 2039) under a general National Archives policy that applied to all federal investigations by the executive branch of government, a period "intended to serve as protection for innocent persons who could otherwise be damaged because of their relationship with participants in the case." As they concluded that Oswald acted alone in killing the president and Ruby acted alone in killing Oswald it doesn't seem to make sense with Ruby's mob connections and the history between the Kennedy's and the mob. Other conspiracy theories were talked about such as the CIA, the FBI, Vice President Johnson, President Castro in Cuba, and the KGB. Chief of Police Jesse Curry said that Oswald had admitted nothing. The FBI informed Dallas police late Friday night that they had the order letter for the rifle found in the Texas Book Depository and the writing on the letter was the same as Oswald's handwriting. Curry was sure he had the man who assassinated the president and he wanted him moved from city jail to county jail. Chief Curry really didn't think someone was going to actually shoot Oswald. The assassination happened right in front of Dallas residents Bill and Gayle Newman and their two young sons. Mr. Newman believe that he heard the shots come from the Book Depository. At first Mrs. Newman thought that the noise was fire crackers. She was never around guns and wouldn't know what they sounded like. Neither one of them actually knew what was going on until the president's motorcade got directly in front of them. That was when the third shot which struck him in his head and made a small explosion. They were questioned later on by the news station in Dallas about what they saw. For those in Dealey Plaza who saw the assassination happen they all knew what was coming out of it. At Parkland doctors desperately try to save Kennedy but hospital officials later said that President Kennedy was medically dead on his way to the hospital. While people across the United States found out as time went on that afternoon that their president died, the country paused and citizens near and far were glued to their televisions. Back home in Hyannis Port at the Kennedy compound Mrs. Rose Kennedy found out about the death of her son. Mrs. Kennedy waited a while before telling her husband Joe about John's death. The Kennedy family and his physician weren't sure he was strong enough to take the shocking news. Mr. and Mrs. Kennedy had lost three of their nine children. As people mourned from all over the country and the world, the country didn't just lose a president but two young children lost a father and our beautiful first lady became a widow at just 34 years old. While the country will never know the reason Kennedy was killed and who was behind his assassination they come to honor President Kennedy at Arlington National Cemetery as the eternal flame stays lit through snow and rain for a fallen hero for over 50 years. One of President Johnson's first acts as the President of the United States was to declare the day of President Kennedy's funeral as a day of mourning. When a new president suddenly took office and the citizens now listen to a man with a southern accent take over the Boston accent they were used to hearing made most of Americans realize John Kennedy was gone. In January 1961 glamour and class was brought into the White House with the president's glamorous wife and two young children Caroline and John Jr., Pennsylvania Avenue and the rest of

Washington D.C. saw nothing other than a new generation as the president said in his inaugural address on that cold January day. As citizens pour into Washington three years later for the funeral of America's president they poured into Washington differently in 1963. Citizens came without smiles, without cheering, and without hope. They stood still silently as the coffin carrying John F. Kennedy was brought through the streets of Washington to the Rotunda of the Capitol Building where all of citizens can come in and pay their respects for the former chief executive. More than 250,000 citizens walked through the capitol building before the doors closed Monday morning as the president is taken to his final resting place. For most people young and old this was almost a fear of what next? Was war going to soon happen? Was someone also trying to kill Lyndon Johnson as well? Did this have to do with the Cuban Missile Crisis just a year before in 1962? These questions feared President Johnson, the secret service, the government, and the United States. Kennedy kept us out of war and maintained a strong relationship with the then Soviet Union after he got Castro and Cuba to back down In October of 1962. After learning that Lee Harvey Oswald had defected to the Soviet Union in 1959 also raised questions for Dallas Police and secret service. Jackie Kennedy walked the streets of Washington behind her husband's casket hoping someone would take a shot at her and kill her. She refused to ride in the car, Caroline and John-John rode in the car with their nanny. Bobby Kennedy and Ted Kennedy both said if she was walking they were walking with her. The three of them walked behind the dead president along with some of President Kennedy's secret service agents and Mrs. Kennedy's secret service agent Clint Hill who remained with Mrs. Kennedy until the election in 1964 when he moved to the Johnson administration. As tragedy once again happened to the Kennedy family, the family began to fear for their children and their grandchildren as they live through tragedy from young ages watching a father, son, husband, and uncle die. As the Kennedy family, America, and the rest of the world suffers this tragic loss of a leader who was a model to all they have to face that they will probably never know as a second assassins bullet silences the alleged assassin. Lee Oswald dies a slow death after being shot by Jack Ruby. As police and detectives wait for an ambulance Oswald lays on the floor lifeless and Jack Ruby is taken by Oswald as he goes upstairs to a jail cell. Oswald is rushed to Parkland

Memorial Hospital where President Kennedy had died just two days earlier. As Oswald is rushed in secret service and officers were screaming in his face "did you do it?" Oswald didn't answer. Doctors ended up opening Oswald's chest and massaging his heart by hand hoping to get a beat. Doctors failed to revive him and Oswald dies just 48 hours and 7 minutes after President Kennedy was killed. As Police Chief Jesse Curry announces to the press at the Dallas city jail that Oswald passed away reporters wanted to know more about Jack Ruby and why yet another shooting happened in Dallas within 48 hours. Hundreds of people waited outside the city jail waiting to get a look at Oswald some heard the shot and others heard that Oswald was fighting for his life. Lots of Dallas residents broke out into a cheer after hearing the alleged assassin was killed. Others believed as most Americans believe today that Oswald's death was extremely regrettable. They believed the dignity of our country would have been preserved if Lee Oswald had the right of trial by jury which is what our 35th President stood for. John F. Kennedy will always be remembered as a kind man, a man who protected his country, who put his people before others, who treated all Americans the same whether their religion, race, or color.

We will remember him simply by his words *"And so my fellow Americans, Ask not what your country can do for you, ask what you can do for your country."*

Chapter 16

The Legacy of JFK

November 22, 1963 America lost its president what began in San Antonio for a five day two speech tour of Texas ended with John F. Kennedy's assassination in Dallas. Who ever thought a young man from Harvard, a young man unprepared for the dangers of war, who becomes captain of his boat and who survived when his boat sank in the Solemn Islands deep in the Pacific? Who ever thought that young man would become President of the United States? That young man was John F. Kennedy, captain of his naval boat PT 109 died tragically but left a legacy behind. John F. Kennedy got elected as the youngest President to ever take office. He had none other than hope and inspiration for his generation and for the 1960's. He inspired that generation to accepted responsibility for their government and the world. His number one act as President was fighting to ensure equal rights and freedom for all Americans. He helped those who were less fortunate, and those who were in danger. He took social and political action as chief executive. Kennedy was president during a time most Americans were nervous about the break of war between the United States and the Soviet Union. The war between Democracy and communism was becoming more of a national problem, seeing that the United States and the Soviet Union possessed enough nuclear weapons to destroy the world. When Kennedy received a threat of Nuclear War with Moscow and Cuba but showed the United States and the world that he was able to get President Castro to back down and in October of 1962 he did just that. Kennedy's civil rights proposals led to the Civil Rights Act of 1964. Kennedy's successor President Lyndon Johnson pushed the Civil Rights Act through a bitterly divided congress by invoking the late president's memory. In Houston, Texas on September 12, 1962 President John Kennedy gave his famous "We choose to go to the Moon" speech. His speech intended to persuade the citizens of the United States to support the Apollo Program. In his speech, Kennedy characterized space as a new frontier, invoking the pioneer spirit that dominated American folklore. When John F. Kennedy took office as the 35th President of the United States, many Americans believed that the United States was losing the space race with the Soviet Union, which had successfully launched the first artificial satellite, Sputnik 1 almost four years earlier. Kennedy stood before Congress on May 25, 1961, and proposed that the US "should commit itself to achieving the goal, before this decade is out, of landing a man on the Moon and returning him safely to the Earth. Kennedy stood before 40,000 people in Houston, Texas on a warm, sunny day September 12, 1962 promising a man would land on a moon before the 1960's were over. Kennedy stated in his speech: "We choose to go to the moon in this decade and do the other things, not because it is easy, but because it is hard; because that goal will serve to organize and measure the best of our energies and skills, because that challenge is one that we are willing to accept, one we are unwilling to postpone, and one we intend to win, and the others, too." The speech resonated widely and is still remembered, although at the time there was disquiet about the cost and value of the Moon-landing effort. Kennedy's goal was realized in July 1969 with the successful Apollo 11 mission. John F. Kennedy loved the media and he knew how to use it to talk to the country. During the 1960 Presidential debate between him and Vice President Richard Nixon, Kennedy looked calm, cool, and collected while on television where Nixon wasn't so relaxed on camera. Their debate was the first presidential debate to be televised. Kennedy also used the media during his presidency and often welcomed them into the oval office to talk about political issues for the country to hear. On September 2, 1963, two months before Kennedy was killed he helped inaugurate network television's first half-hour nightly evening news with an interview with CBS News Anchor Walter Cronkite. During the "Camelot era" Kennedy and his young family brought joy to the White House and the nation. The term Camelot came to be used as reportedly iconic of the Kennedy administration. The term was used by his wife during an interview with Life Magazine after Kennedy's assassination in Dallas. Mrs. Kennedy stated, "There'll be great presidents again... but there will never be another Camelot." Kennedy had a lot on his agenda starting back in 1960 when he won the election. He had big plans to keep the country safe and big plans to help move the country in the right direction during the 1960's. President Kennedy didn't finish everything he wanted to and never had the chance to take on new tasks in 1964, but his legacy lives on in his family and this country. John Fitzgerald Kennedy died too soon leaving a family behind, a legacy behind, and yet another tragedy in the Kennedy family. He ran for president for his older brother Joe who had bold political aspirations at a young age and was ready to enter politics after his military service. He was going to run for office in his father's place after Joe Kennedy's political career ended when he was ambassador to Great Britain. It was a gift for America that he ran for office. It was a breath of fresh air, and the beginning of a new era, a new generation, and a new frontier as Kennedy said at his inauguration. People came to honor Kennedy and his legacy in Washington, November 25, 1963 as they said good-bye to a true American hero who only cared about his country and people. Today millions of people still honor him and his legacy he left behind him. Now he is a legend, and no one will ever forget the man who became the King of Camelot.

Some of My Family Members and where they were when they heard the news

My Papa (14-years old in 1963) my papa was walking home from Nathan Hale School in New Britain, CT and a lady came out of her house screaming President Kennedy's dead. Then on his way home he stopped at the Farm Shop to call his mom to see what was going on. She told him to come home the news was on with reports that President Kennedy had died.

My Grandma (14-years-old in 1963) my grandma was in junior high school and the teachers were talking about that President Kennedy had been shot. And when she was getting out of school the teachers told everyone the president was dead. Then everyone was talking about it when they were walking home from school.

My great-grandma (36-years-old in 1963) my nana was vacuuming her den and her show was interrupted and a News Bulletin said President Kennedy had been shot. Then she continued to watch the news to see what was going on and after she found out that Kennedy had died.

My great-grandma (42-years-old in 1963) my nana heard on the news that President Kennedy had been shot, she was watching my uncle who was 4 years old at the time. After it was announced that Kennedy was dead my uncle went all around the neighborhood from door to door to tell everyone that the president was dead.

My great-aunt (48-years-old in 1963) my great-aunt Faye lived until she was 103 years old. I asked her where she was when President Kennedy died and she told me she was washing her windows and she had the radio on and it had said that President Kennedy died and she cried like a baby she told me. She loved the Kennedy family and still couldn't believe the assassination of John F. Kennedy really happened years later. She said it was a day no one forgot. She remembered President Kennedy's death until she died in July of 2018 at 103 years old.

My Reaction to Kennedy's Assassination

At 15 years old you are into sports, crafts, school activities, going to different places because you are at the age where you can do things with your friends besides hanging out at each other's houses. I don't know if many teenagers are into history or certain parts of our history. On a November weekend before Thanksgiving in 2013 I was 15 years old and a freshman in high school. My favorite subjects were history and English class. Writing was always one of my big strengths. My dad and I sometimes watch the history channel. We were watching it that November weekend and there were specials on about Kennedy's assassination and the conspiracy theories. I was getting more and more interested as I continued to watch it. I asked a lot of questions, my dad liked my interest in it however, he doesn't remember the assassination and didn't know much about the details, but I later asked my grandparents and aunts and uncles who lived through it and their stories were interesting. I then went and watched the video of Kennedy being shot and it was something I never seen before. It was a piece of history that I realized I never learned about in school. As I look back on all my years in school I really never learned about the presidents and first ladies. We weren't taught details like Lincoln's assassination and then President Garfield, and McKinley's assassination, or Kennedy's. They didn't teach us about Pearl Harbor in 1941 or President Reagan's assassination attempt. I didn't learn much about what some of our great president's went through and accomplished during their administrations. Part of that was why I chose to write this book to encourage teenagers and adults to read about a piece of our nation's history. I watched documentary after documentary and looked at all the conspiracy theories behind the assassination and who could have been involved. There were theories that I never even thought of and others that seemed to make sense. One thing I did as I did my own little investigation on Kennedy's assassination was I kept going back to learn more about Jack Ruby. I thought the Dallas police had enough evidence to tie Oswald to the crime and with his background with Cuba and the Soviet Union made me question about him being the possible suspect. I wondered why he acted so strange when he left work after the assassination happened without telling anyone and went home to grab his pistol and a jacket. He left home rather quickly as well and was avoiding the police which was odd to me. It was odd that he shot the Dallas Police officer who only tried talking to him. All of the things Oswald did was strange in general. He claimed he was a patsy and he probably was. Oswald looked guilty, not just for murder but for anything. After Oswald was silenced by Dallas nightclub owner Jack Ruby I started to focus on him and the kind of person he was. I got the hint that he loved being the center of attention and later learned he was connected with the mob. Let's be serious, no one in this world will ever know what happened on that day in Dallas, Texas. There are so many conspiracy theories and people all over the world believe different ones. It is all in what you believe. Out of all the conspiracy theories about President Kennedy's assassination I believe the Mafia had to do with his murder, along with Marilyn Monroe's death, Martin Luther King's death, and Bobby Kennedy's death. JFK's father Joseph Kennedy had connections with the mob and had Sam Giancana one of America's biggest mobsters help him get John elected president. The Kennedy's and the mob had history. At just 34 years old JFK appoints his younger brother Bobby Kennedy as his attorney general. There was no doubt Bobby Kennedy was JFK's closest and most trusted ally. As attorney general Bobby Kennedy started the organized crime when he decided to go after Sam Giancana and other big mobsters such as Jimmy Hoffa and others. This made Giancana made and he told his buddy Frank Sinatra who was also friends with John F. Kennedy to tell Kennedy to back off if he knows what's good for him. Kennedy didn't and was determined he can get these guys. His determination made his father nervous. Joe Kennedy tried to convince Jack and Bobby to start off small, but they didn't. With JFK's assassination in 1963 and Bobby's assassination five years later, it seems reasonable it was in the result of a conspiracy with the Mafia. They planned it the way it seemed to work by having both brothers killed but apart from each other. However Bobby Kennedy was the leader of the organized crime and if they had him murdered when he was attorney general it wouldn't help that John Kennedy was still president and can continue the organized crime if he wanted to. The mafia or whoever had Kennedy killed knew Bobby would leave office after his brother's death. Which was what ended up happening, Bobby Kennedy and Lyndon Johnson couldn't stand each other there was always tension when they were in the same room and the whole Kennedy administration knew that. John F. Kennedy was killed making Lyndon Johnson president and Bobby wasn't staying in the Johnson administration, so Bobby left the cabinet nine months after his brother's death. Making both Kennedy brothers out of office. Then when Bobby Kennedy entered the campaign race for president, well you can say whoever wanted John Kennedy dead also didn't want Bobby Kennedy president as well. Bobby Kennedy campaigned in the 1968 Presidential Campaign, he campaigned in Los Angeles, California on June 5, 1968 that ended with his assassination a subject that was as shocking as his brothers five years earlier. Jack Ruby was also friends with Sam Giancana. With the president traveling to Texas and Jack Ruby owning two businesses there, I believe Ruby was set up to silence Oswald. I believe that Kennedy was killed because of a conspiracy and I believe the Warren Commission was dead wrong. They told the country what they wanted to hear. I not only learned about Kennedy's assassination but was also interested in his life, and his presidency. He faced a lot of health problems at a young age like his back, he had back surgery when he was senator and slipped into a coma because of it. He suffered from Addison's disease and had digestive problems. His doctors told him to eat as much dairy products as possible to help him gain weight and usually to settle his stomach he had a soothing glass of milk. President Kennedy was very rich and a great president. I enjoy listening to his speeches and how he handled the government. He was the youngest president ever elected and the first Roman Catholic as well. I admired everything about him and especially enjoy listening to his inaugural speech which was probably one of the best inaugural speeches of all time. Although he faced and went through tragedy and also died tragically I often wonder what the country would have been like if he lived. What would his kids be like growing up with their father? Where would we stand as people in the United States if he had another four years in office? These questions not only go through people who lived through the Kennedy presidency but other people who didn't as well. I am one of those people, and like everyone else I can only look back on what was Camelot. My biggest question is of all is what was Oswald's reason to shoot Kennedy? There is enough evidence to tie him to the assassination.

Why did he deny everything? Why are we left with no answers more than five decades later?

John Fitzgerald Kennedy

May 29, 1917 – November 22, 1963

United States Congressman from Massachusetts:

January 3, 1947 – January 3, 1953

United States Senator from Massachusetts:

January 3, 1953 – December 22, 1960

35th President of the United States:

January 20, 1961 – November 22, 1963

United States Navy:

1941 – 1945

About the Author

I just was 15 years old when I became so very interested in President John F. Kennedy and his assassination. I was like any other person in America. I wanted to know why it happened and how. I was a freshman in high school and very interested in history, I always thought it is so important to not only learn about our nation's history but to honor it, remember it, and cherish it. I was not here in 1963, I cannot say I lived through Kennedy's presidency or his assassination. However, I honor and quite often think about him and his beautiful family and smile because I am very lucky to have a big family like he did. In my civics class in freshman year we talked a lot about the presidents and the important roles they play not only for their country but for the future of their country. I learned when you elect a president even if it was the president you didn't vote for. You simply take it day by day, month by month, and year by year to see what he or she will accomplish. It could help the country or it could simply not help the country but as long as whatever the president does doesn't affect me personally and I am living my life I simply think to myself it can be much worse. When I became interested in

Kennedy's assassination and decided myself to research it and see where my opinion falls I also became interested in not only the person he was but the president he was. How he spoke during his speeches, how he handled conflict, how he appeared on television, and how he persuade his country. I sat down watching a show on conspiracy theories about his assassination. A lot of them made sense and I became more and more into it. Then I decided to watch move movies, documentaries, read books, researched, and wrote papers about his assassination and who I think did it and who I thought was involved. It got to the point where not only my family and friends even my teachers in school saw my obsession about it and the support and compliments they all have given me is truly unbelievable. My teachers gave me magazines and books they found on Kennedy. My friends and family bought me lots of Kennedy related souvenirs, pictures, books, old newspapers from 1963, etc. Since I was a kid I had always been interested in history and didn't realize how much Kennedy's assassination changed history forever until I learned more about it and what it did to our country. I was so interested I researched about it during my breaks in school, when I got home from school, and on the weekends. In my sophomore year of high school I decided to write a book about the assassination and share my conspiracy theories with the people of the world. I wrote it and forgot about it. I was in high school and wasn't sure whether to publish it or not. I later realized my big passion in life is to write. As far as president's go Kennedy is one of my favorites. My freshman year of college I found it in my computer and decided to edit it and publish it for the public to see. Reading is very important and also a tool we all use though not many young kids see it as a tool most adults do and teenagers who become adults. I realized what reading can do and it is a wonderful thing. Not many kids and young teens are interested in history like that but I am proud to say I am and that I found it interesting to study and research on. I think History is very important and that it is very important that we know what actually happened to our former Chief Executive. I believe President Kennedy, his alleged assassin Lee Oswald, his brother Robert, Martin Luther King Jr., and Marilyn Monroe were all killed as the result of conspiracies by the Mafia. We will never find out if it really was or who was involved. And many citizens believe different things. My theory is the Mob I truly believe it was. Here is my book with what happened to our beloved 35th President of the United States John F. Kennedy and what I think from my research. It's the story of the tragic end of what was known as Camelot. Whether you are interested in history or not I encourage everyone to read this book for just one reason to simply learn and think about a piece of history that happened to our country, our government, a family, and the rest of the world. Most of us know this sense of tragic as most of us lived through September 11th and we still to this day remember, honor, and pay respects to all those who tragically lost their lives. I wrote this book to simply help kids, teenagers, and adults read a little something about a shocking event that happened. Every person who I have asked about November 22, 1963 has never forgotten where they were, what they were doing, who they were with, and how they found out. Even decades later it's simply a day that no one can ever forget. I hope all Americans and the rest of the world enjoys this book with a piece of our nation's history and a historic family. They were a family everyone knew by last name. Whether anyone enjoys history or not or enjoys this book or not I hope after whoever reads my book that they will learn and remember an important part of our nation's history, it isn't a bad thing to keep it in the back of your mind but simply think about a piece of information that you can share with someone else about one of our nation's most famous presidents in presidential history. I know history isn't something every child, teenager or even adult is interested in. I was once never interested in history or anything that happened before my time. I was just three years old on September 11, 2001. I remember my mother turning the news on and being in shock but whatever it was didn't seem to faze three year old me. I learned about September 11th each year in school and how it affected our country and President Bush and it made me realize what the nation went through on that tragic day in New York. After learning as a teenager about the Kennedy Assassination I didn't realize until watching that famous film taking by Abraham Zappruder in Dealey Plaza that day what Mrs. Kennedy had to see and go through from watching her husband's head be blown off right in front of her to laying him to rest three days later. It was something every American paused and paid respects to as they watched the president be carried to his grave at Arlington National Cemetery. As we approach November 22nd each year anyone old enough will recall that moment with vivid clarity. It was a day so shocking people all over the country and around the world still remember where they were and what they were doing when news came out that JFK had been killed. The Kennedy Assassination is nothing but history and we as American's were left with an unanswered question. Who killed John F. Kennedy?

There will never be another Camelot or a true patriot like John F. Kennedy. He kept his nation out of war, and constantly put his citizens first regardless, of race, religion, or politics. For millions of Americans, his way of running our country was like a professional without competition. John Kennedy died too soon and is still in many hearts of this nation. Camelot was a family graced with beauty and fabulous wealth, but also suffered from tragedies. Today they are remembered as one of the nations most loved political families ever. The family faced two assassinations, four plane crashes, a failed lobotomy, and the Chappaquiddick incident in July of 1969. Their lives were simply questionable. They were Kennedy's.

John Fitzgerald Kennedy
the 35th President of the United States
May 29, 1917 – November 22, 1963

Made in the USA
Middletown, DE
07 November 2019